GUITAR
EASY
RECORDED VERSIONS

WITH NOTES
AND TABLATURE

THE VAUGHAN BROTHERS

Family Style

© Kim Upton

Hal Leonard Publishing Corporation
7777 West Bluemound Road P.O. Box 13819 Milwaukee, WI 53213

ISBN 0-7935-0796-0

INTRODUCTION

This book is for the less experienced player who wants to get into the music of the Vaughan Brothers, Jimmie and Stevie Ray, and their monumental album "Family Style." Obviously, it would be difficult for anyone who is just starting out on guitar to play this material. We have created this publication to fill just such a void, for the young player who is looking for exciting, accurate, and challenging music.

Presented here are off-the-record chord voicings and licks, along with introductory lessons for each song, written by experienced players who have studied this music. For more of the Vaughan Brothers, check out the authentic note-for-note Guitar Recorded Version (HL00694776). For more of Stevie Ray Vaughan, check out the authentic note-for-note Guitar Recorded Versions of "In Step," (HL00660136) and "Lightnin' Blues 1983-1987," (HL00660058).

HARD TO BE

LESSON

Throughout this book, you will notice that some songs are notated in standard tuning (E A D G B E), while others indicate to tune down 1/2 step (E♭ A♭ D♭ G♭ B♭ E♭). This is how they were recorded, but at times you may find it more practical to maintain one tuning. If you choose standard tuning, songs written in E♭ tuning will sound 1/2 step higher than the recording, while E♭ tuning will make those written in standard tuning 1/2 step lower.

"Hard To Be" is a Lonnie Mack style rave-up that features a driving rhythm figure imbedded with Chuck Berryisms. Skip the intro lick (bar 1) until you've got a firm grasp on the rhythm part. Follow these steps:

1. Play the 7th position B^5 chord (root and 5th step of B) for the first two eighth notes ("one and...") using downstrokes of the pick throughout.

2. Stretch your pinky to the 11th fret G# (6th scale step of B) to create the B^6 chord for the next eighth note. ("Two")

3. Play the B root only for the eighth note on the "2nd" of 2.

4. Stretch your pinky way up to the 12th fret A note (the all-important "blue" 7th scale step of B) for the following two eighth notes ("3-and").

5. Beat four contains two eighth notes that retrace your steps in reverse, descending on the B^6 and B^5 chords respectively.

Start slowly and patiently build up the tempo. Once you can get this pattern flowing you've got most of the tune licked! The rest of the rhythm figure simply involves position switching and string-jumping.

The instrumental melody in the Intro and after the first Verse is a short but sweet 2-bar statement repeated 4x and can teach you a lot about slurring and phrasing. After the first Verse, you can continue playing the part labeled Rhythm Figure 1, or you can come right out of the rhythm part into the solo melody. Here's how:

1. Play the 9th fret F# (common to the B^5 chord in the rhy. fig.) with your 3rd finger.

2. After picking the 2nd F# slide in tempo up a whole step to G# at the 11th fret and the remaining notes in the 9th positon. Remember, position is named by the location of your fretting-hand index finger.

The slurred grace notes (top) in the 3rd phrase add a jazzy touch before the final 2 bar restatement.

Also of note is Stevie Ray Vaughan's Albert-King inspired reverse-raked grace-slide across two or more high strings which both men frequently use as a percussive rhythmic accent.

Hard To Be

By Stevie Ray Vaughan and Doyle Bramhall

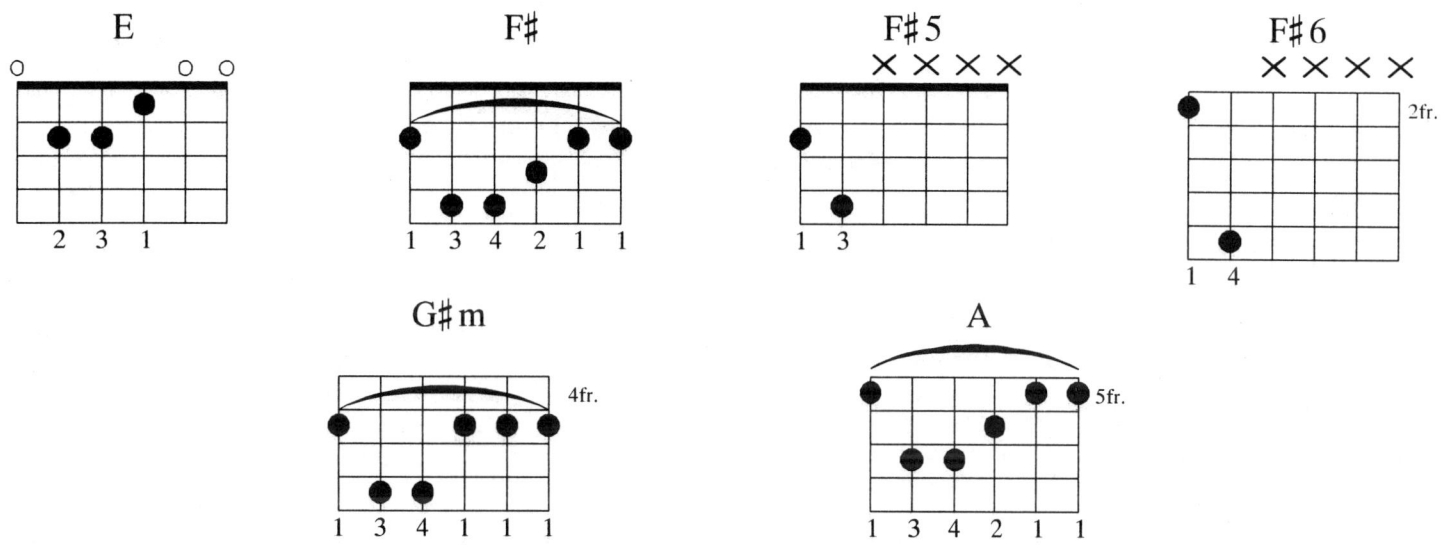

Tune Down 1/2 Step

④=Db ①=Eb
⑤=Ab ②=Bb
⑥=Eb ③=Gb

Intro

a tempo

Moderately Fast Rock ♩=158

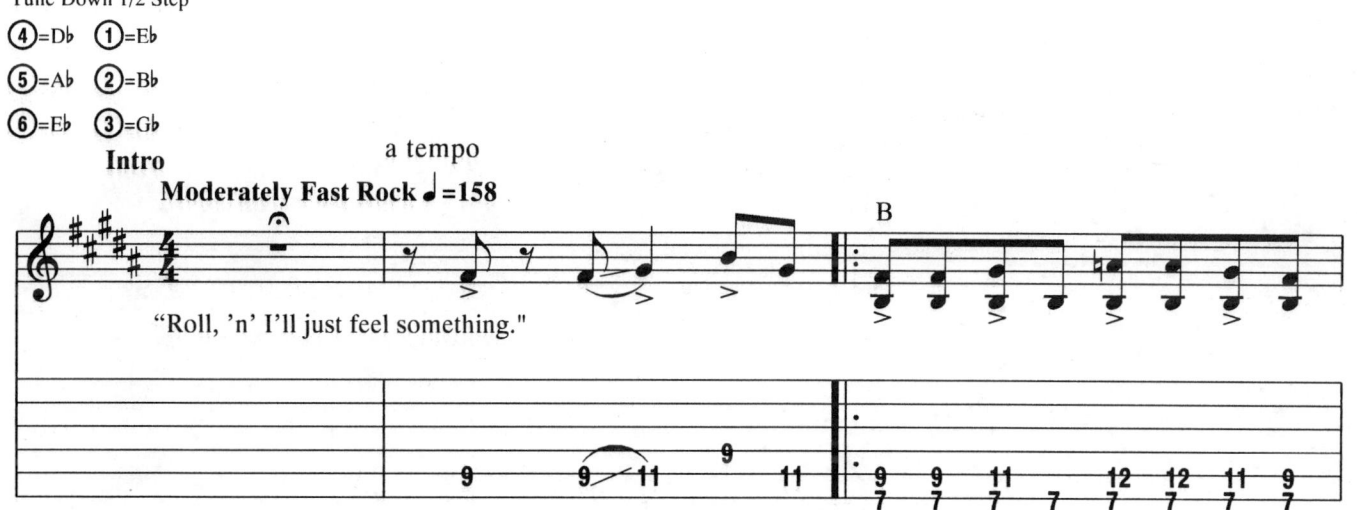

"Roll, 'n' I'll just feel something."

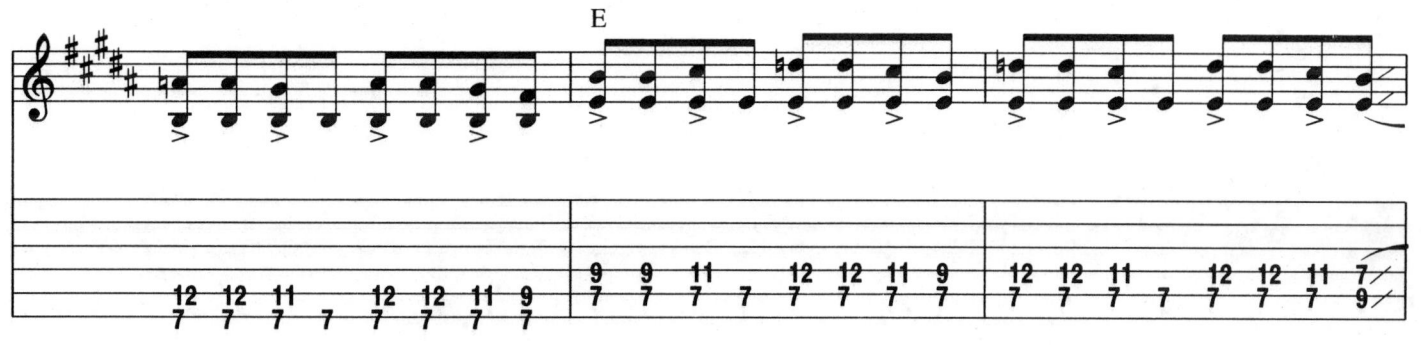

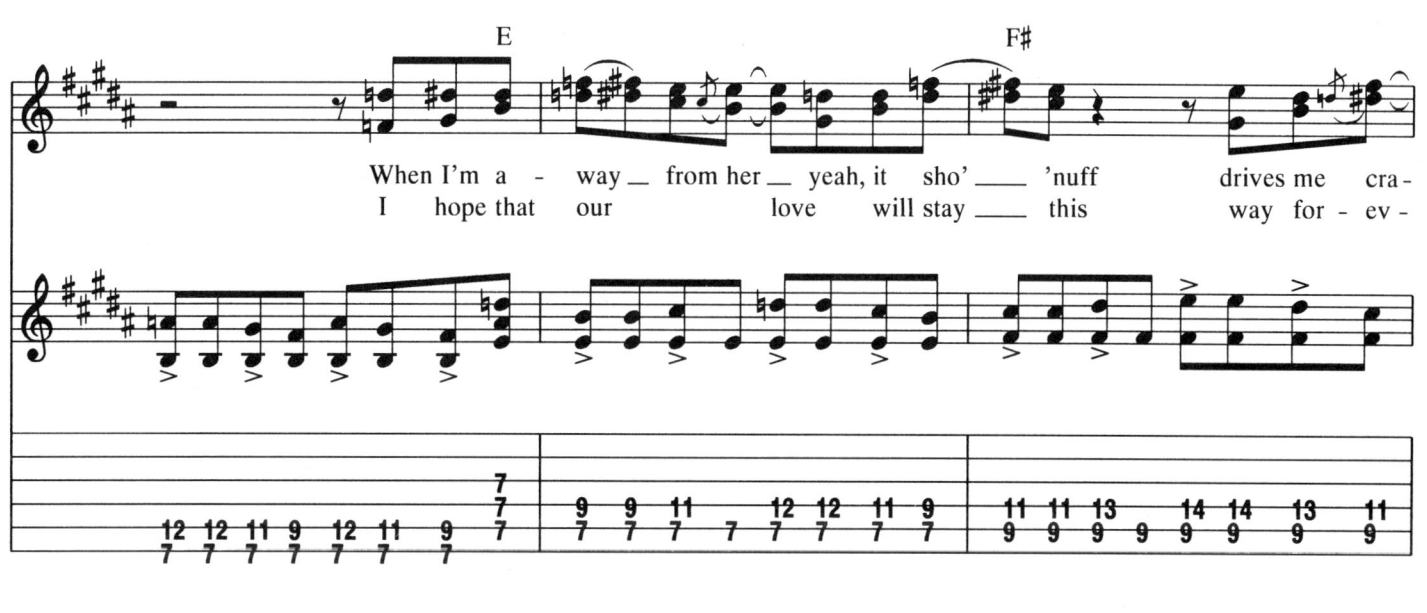

When I'm a - way ___ from her ___ yeah, it sho' ___ 'nuff drives me cra -

I hope that our ___ love ___ will stay ___ this way for - ev -

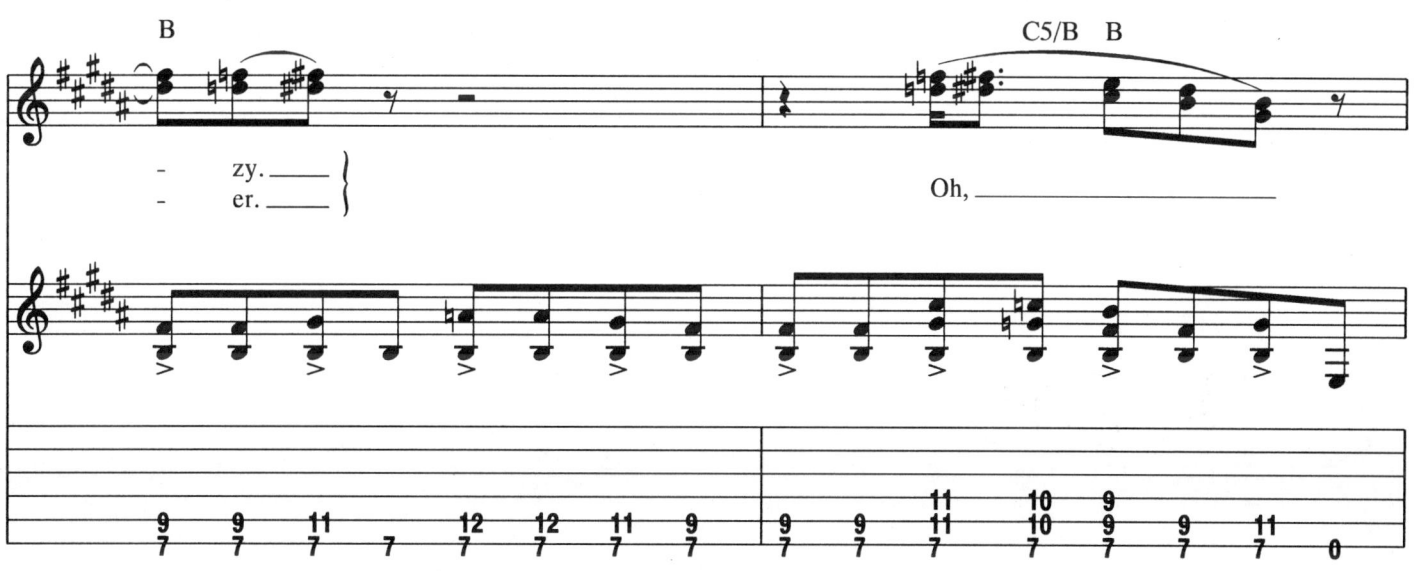

- zy. ___

- er. ___

Oh, _____

some-thin' in - side ___ of me, ___ when she's gone, I

miss her so. _____ I wan - na tell her

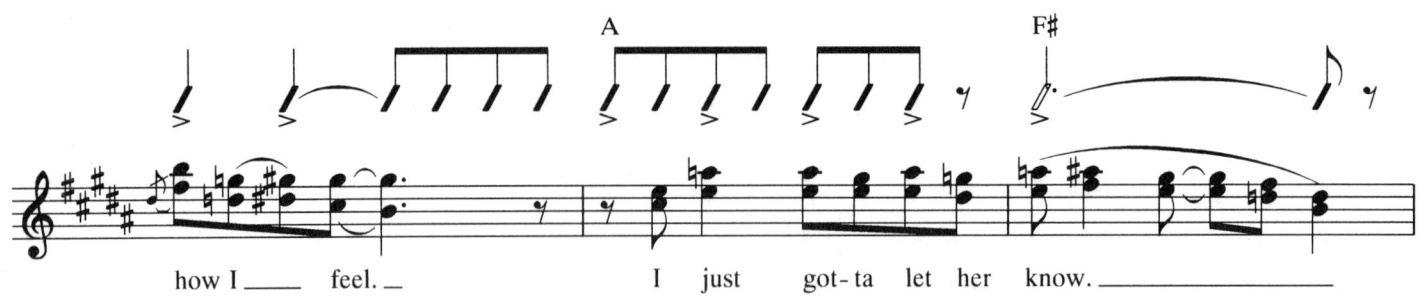

how I ____ feel. _____ I just got-ta let her know. _____

1.,3. When I'm all a - lone ___ with her, ___
2. Look-in' through _ her eyes, _ I see par - a - dise.
and she's in _
No mis-

___ my arms, ___ I'm in heav - en. ___
take she's ___ full ___ of _____ fire. ___

|1.

Well, like a real live __ wire, __ a house on fire, __ she's my burn-

- in', she's my burn - in', burn - in' de - sire. _____

2. It's

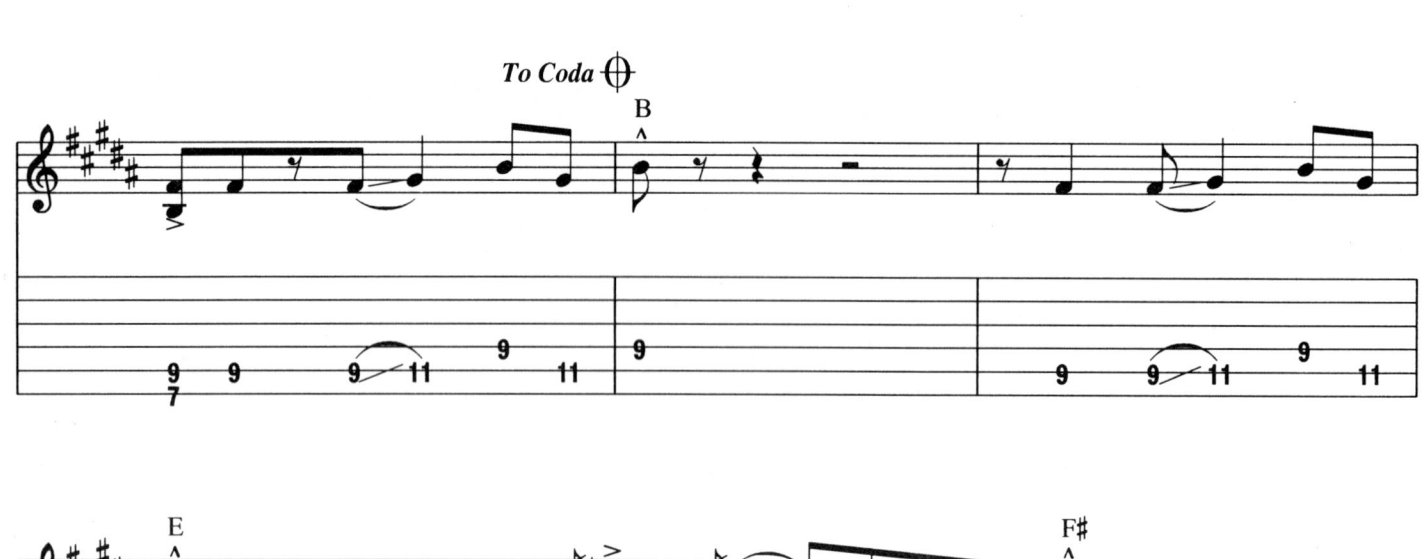

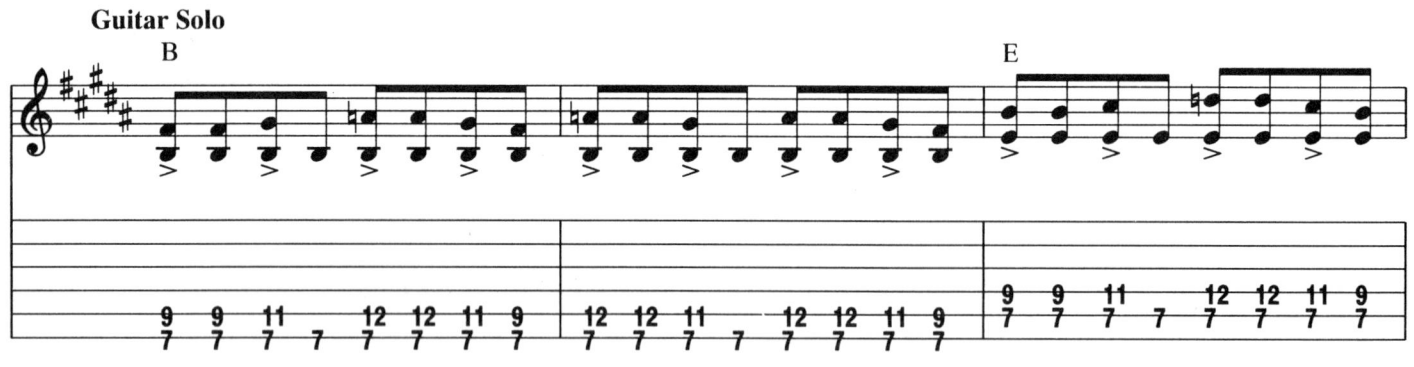

3. Well it's

 **Coda**

Hard to be, ___ *(it's ___ so ___) hard for me. ___

*Cue notes and parenthesised worlds on repeat only

It's hard ___ to keep, ___ keep ___ me from my ba -

- by. Hard to be, ___

WHITE BOOTS

LESSON

A funky outing in standard tuning, "White Boots" originally featured a 6-string Danelectro bass in the rhythm guitar role. You can check this part out during the guitar solo section where it has been arranged for standard 6-string.

First, the short, almost "Proud Mary"-like Intro sets up a main groove (beginning at bar 7) which continues throughout the tune. Here we'll concentrate on the acoustic guitar part notated in rhythm slashes above the vocal line. Be sure to discern between the two types of accents used: > indicates a normal accent note while V is used for short, staccato accents.

When playing extended strumming patterns, it's extremely important to maintain a strong, even sense of time. Use your picking arm as a timekeeping aid by playing alternate down (⊓) and up (V) strokes synchronized with the eighth note pulse, in this case. (The same concept is often applied to 16th note grooves.) When a chord or note is not picked, follow through with inaudible pickstrokes until the next picked event. This will automatically fall on the "correct" down or up stroke. In the following example, the inaudible pickstrokes are shown in parenthesis.

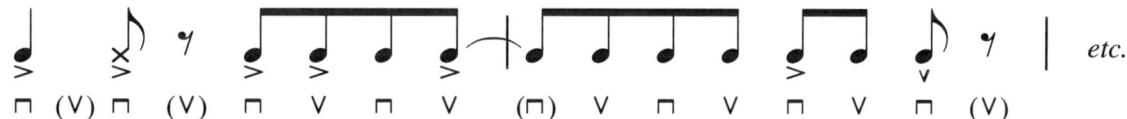

Of course, musical rules often beg to be broken. Sometimes this isn't the right tool for the job and an all-downstrokes approach yields better results, as in "Hard To Be".

For the 2nd Guitar Solo, the G-string bass part has been arranged in standard tuning. Learn the 2-bar figure in the 3rd position first. The remainder of the progression simply involves moving the "shape" to other positions: 5th for E and open for B.

The Coda features a repeating 4-bar progression beginning at bar 66. Note how the root of the E chord is often anticipated on the "and" of beat 4 to push the rhythm and facilitate easier chord switching.

White Boots

By Billy Swan and Jim Leslie

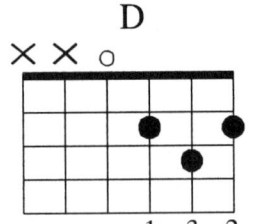
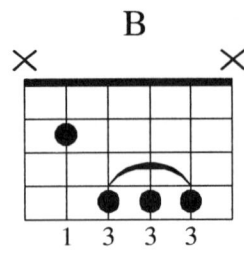
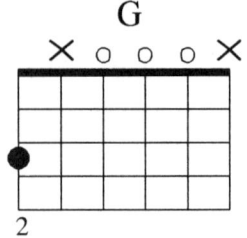
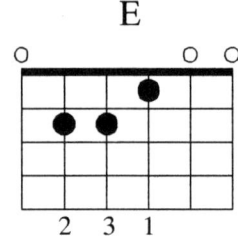

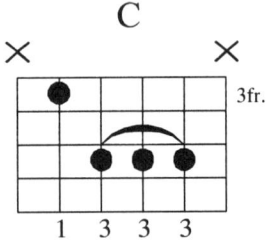
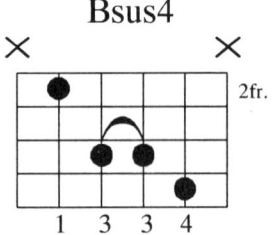

Intro
Moderately Fast Rock ♩=146

Ah white boots, ___ yeah. ___

Acous. Gtr.

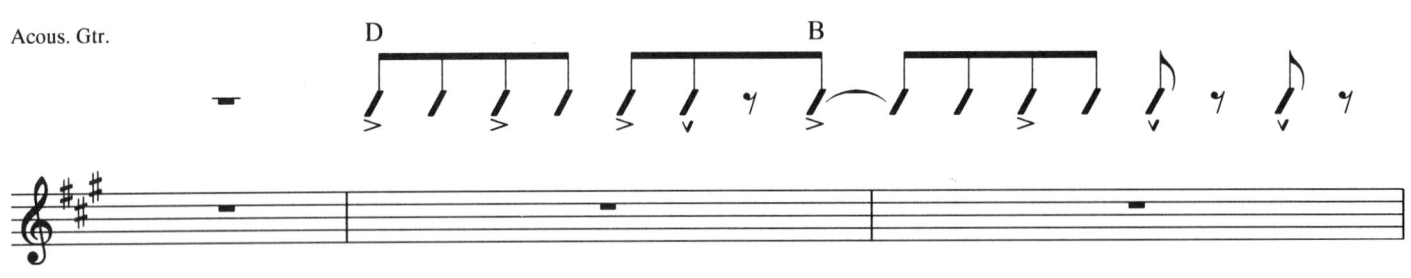

Verse

Ah, that's my ba-by in the white boots. ___

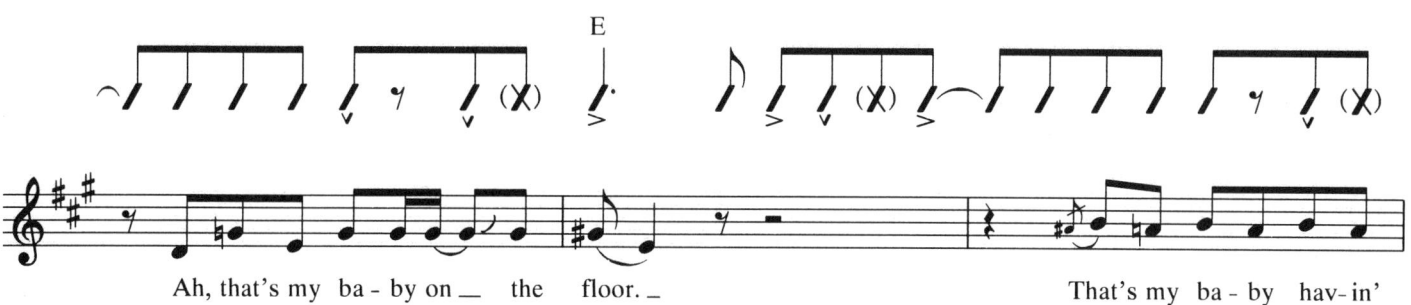

Ah, that's my ba - by on __ the floor. __ That's my ba - by hav - in'

some __ fun, _____ and yell - in' more, __ more, __ more. __

That's my ba - by in the short skirt, _ woo, _____ out of con - trol. _
2. so good. _ You know, I can't ex - plain, _
3. white boots. _ That's my ba - by on the

Ah, she be - comes an - oth - er wom - an, _
how when she's danc - in' in the white boots, _
floor. _ That's my ba - by hav - in' some fun, _

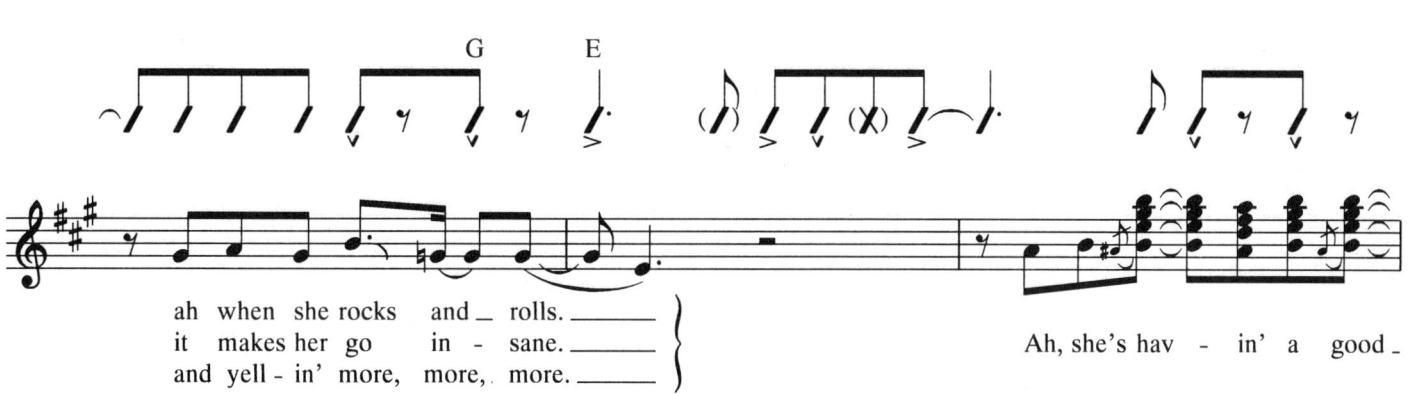

ah when she rocks and __ rolls. _____
it makes her go in - sane. _____
and yell - in' more, more, more. _____

Ah, she's hav - in' a good _

time, go-in' 'round and round.

She's real-ly rip-pin' it up. You know she can't sit down,

To Coda ⊕

oh, no. {That's my ba-by look-in' / That's my ba-by in the short skirt.

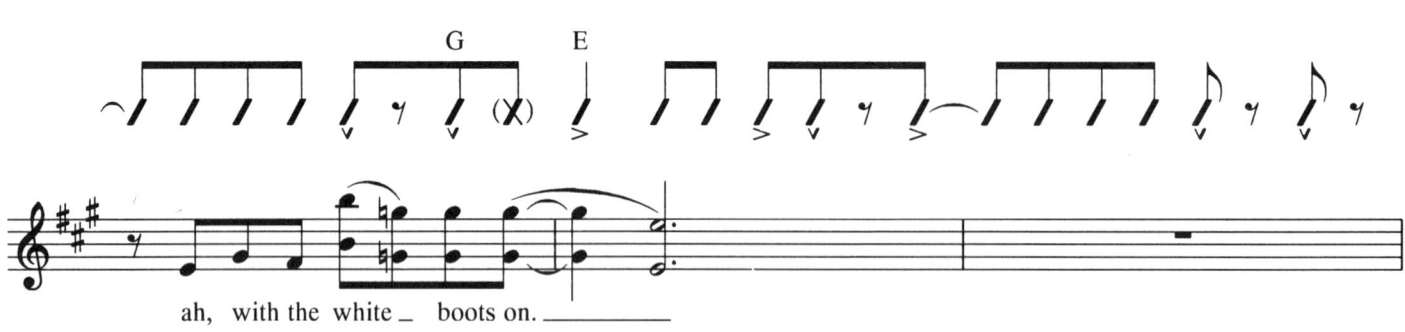

ah, with the white boots on.

Guitar Solo

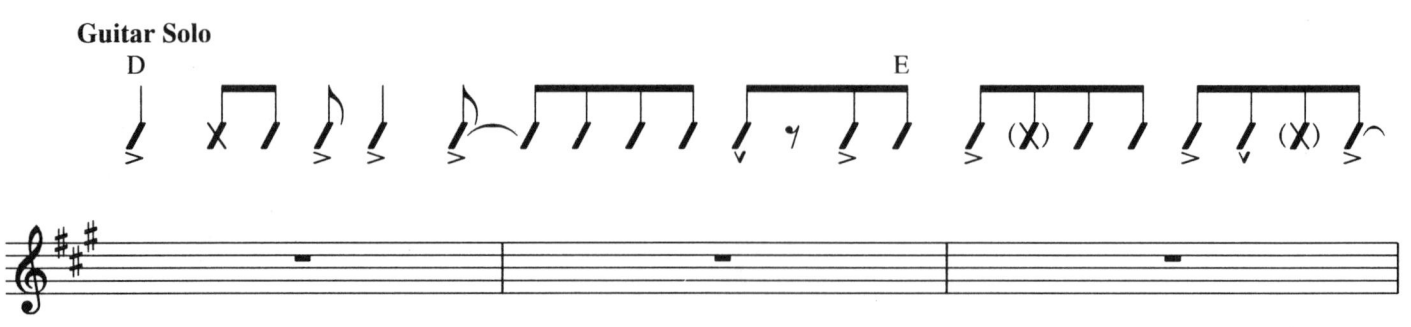

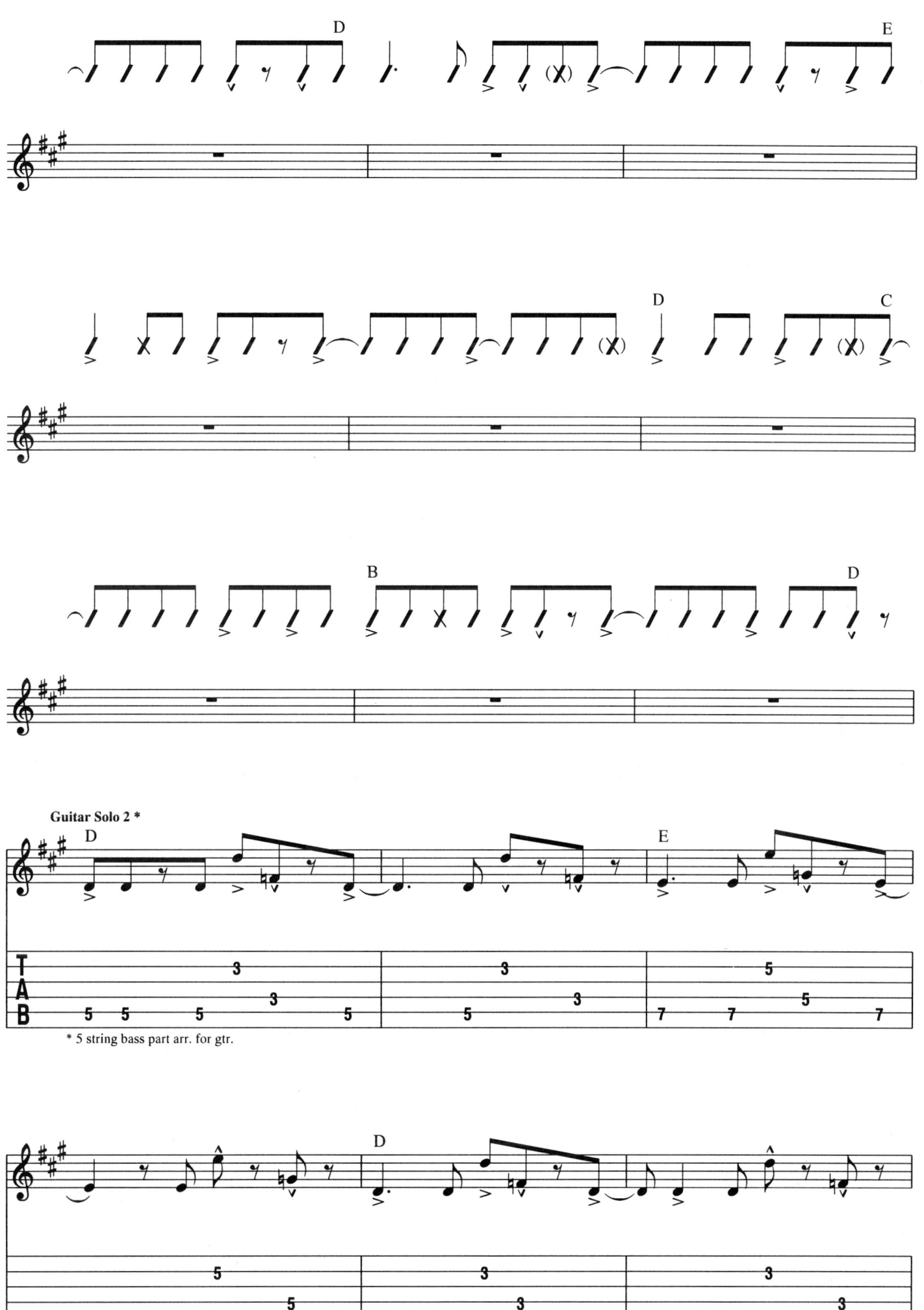

* 5 string bass part arr. for gtr.

D.S. al Coda

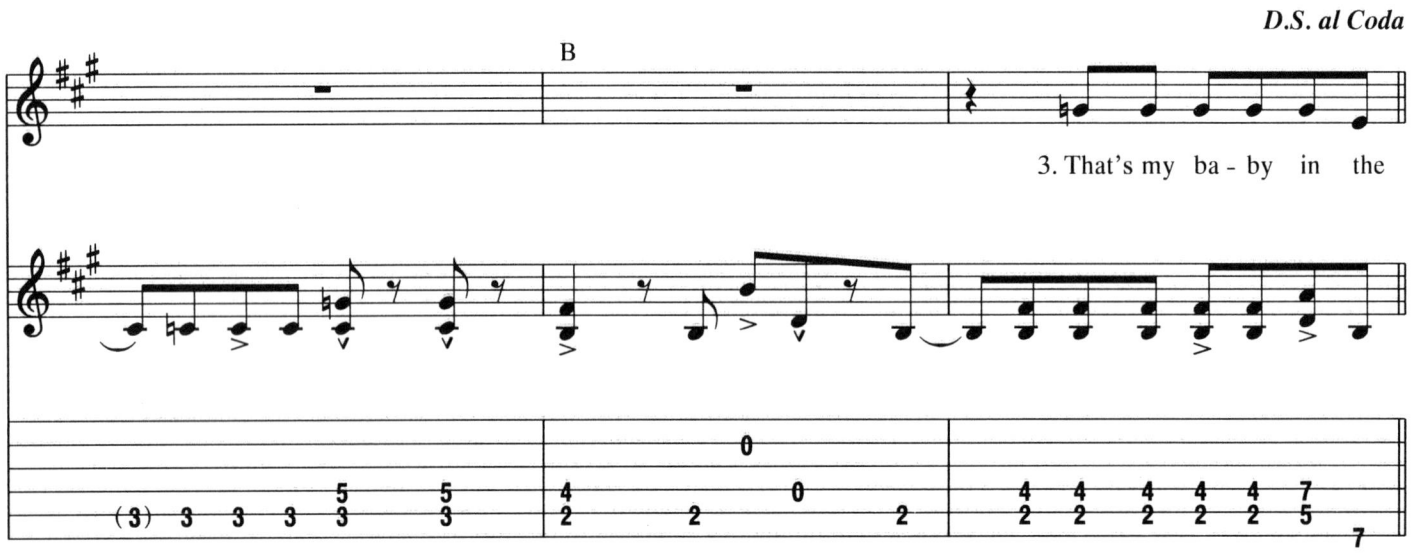

3. That's my ba - by in the

⊕ *Coda*

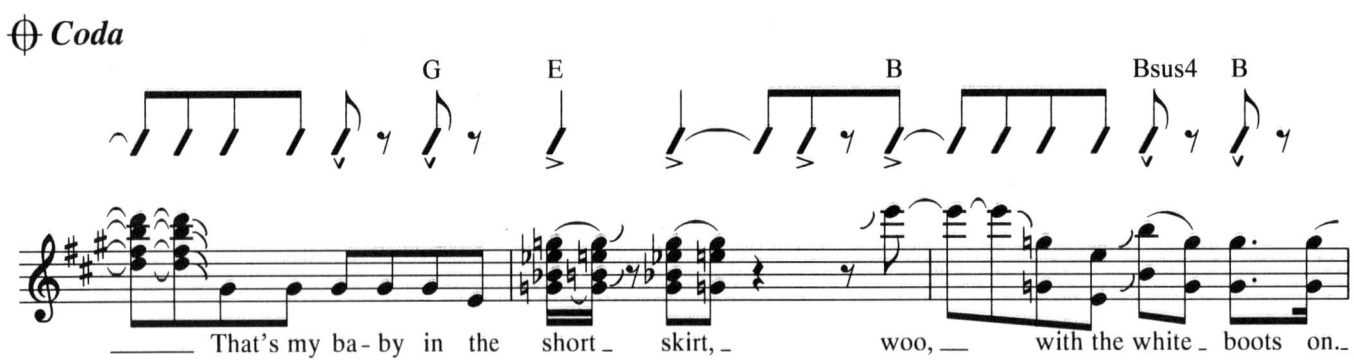

_____ That's my ba - by in the short _ skirt, _ woo, _ with the white _ boots on._

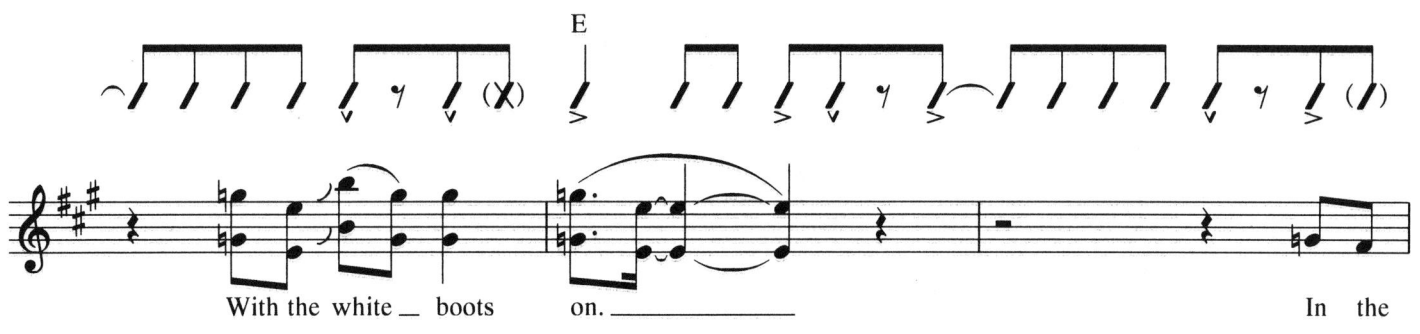

With the white _ boots on. _____ In the

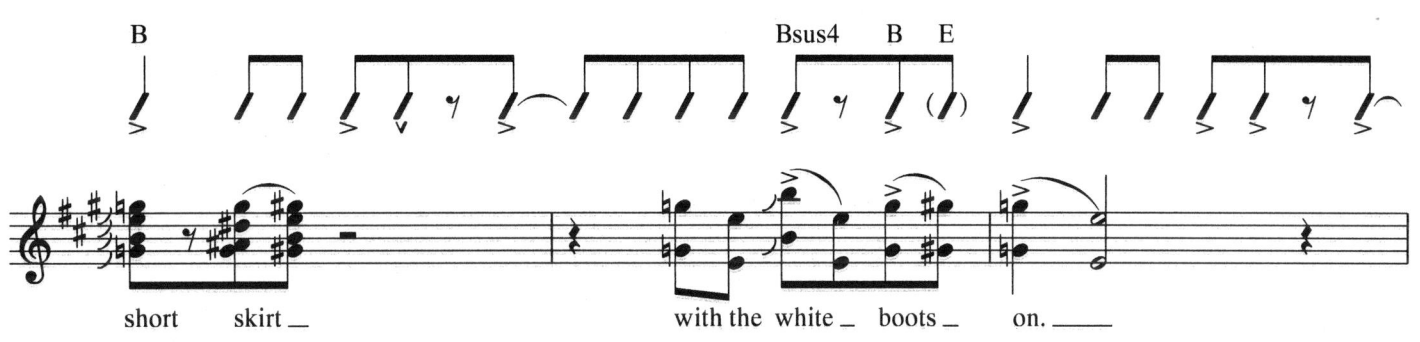

short skirt _ with the white _ boots _ on. ____

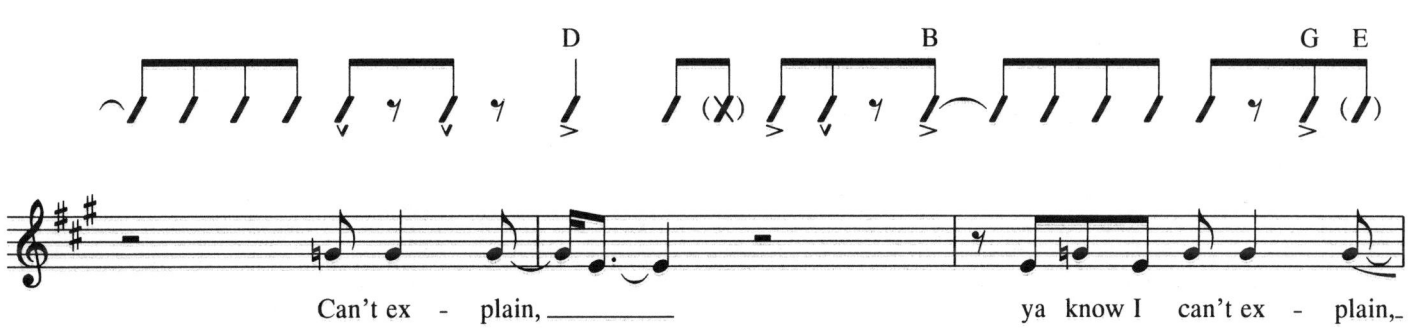

Can't ex - plain, _____ ya know I can't ex - plain, _

_____ how when she's danc-in' in the white _ boots, _

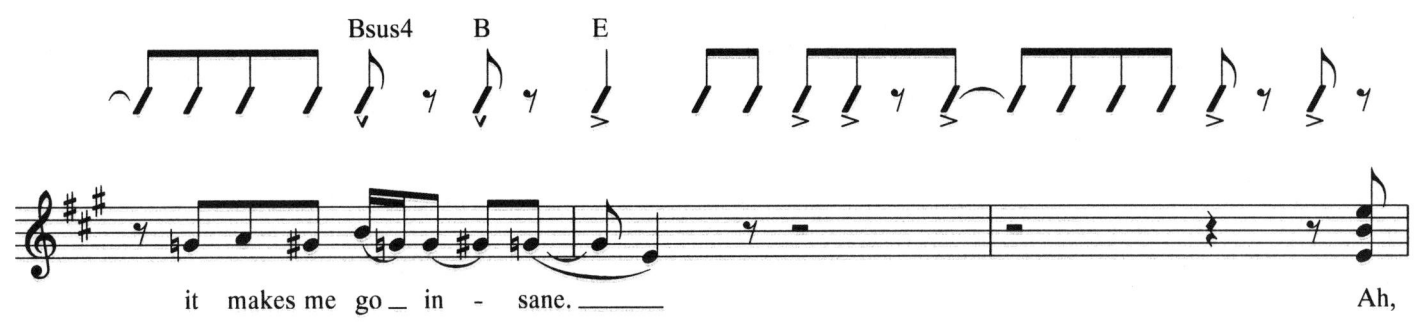

it makes me go in - sane. _____ Ah,

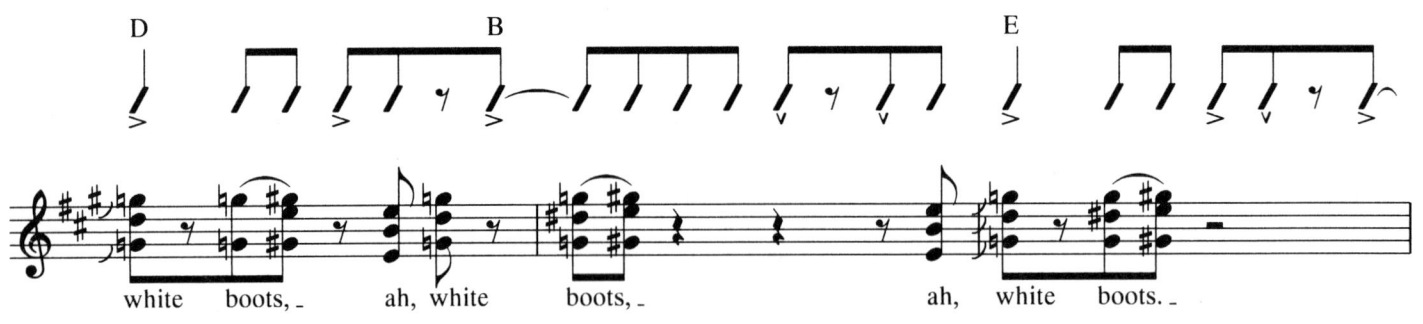

white boots, _ ah, white boots, _ ah, white boots.

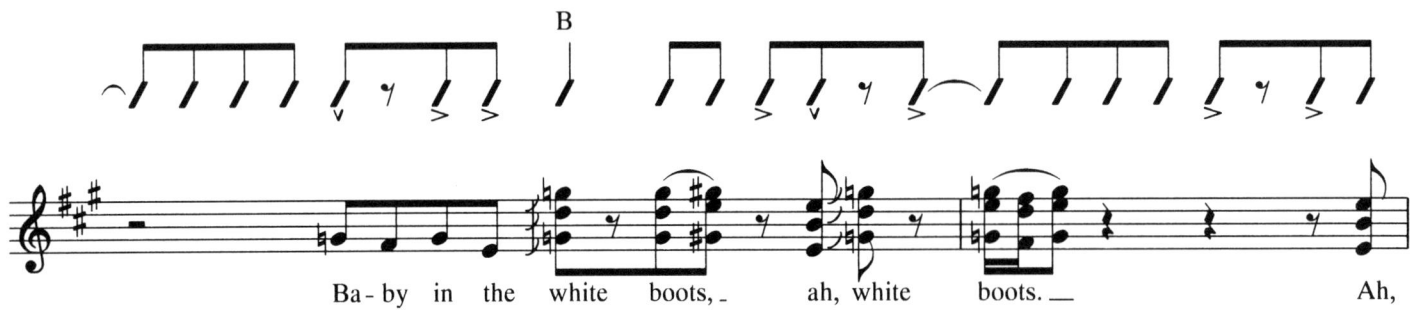

Ba-by in the white boots, _ ah, white boots. _ Ah,

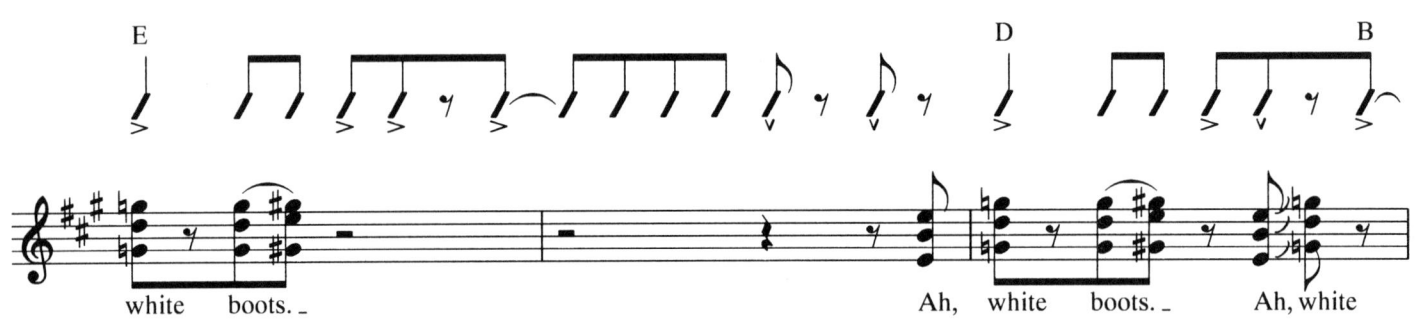

white boots. _ Ah, white boots. _ Ah, white

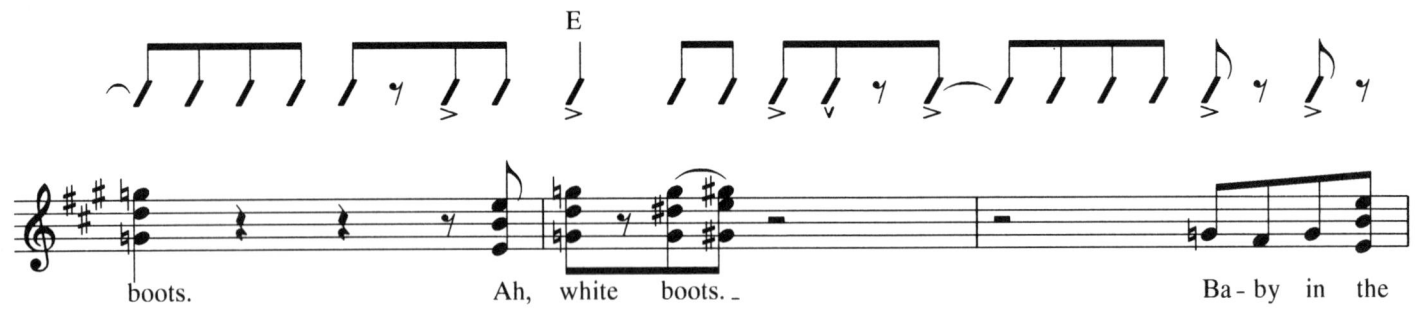

boots. Ah, white boots. _ Ba-by in the

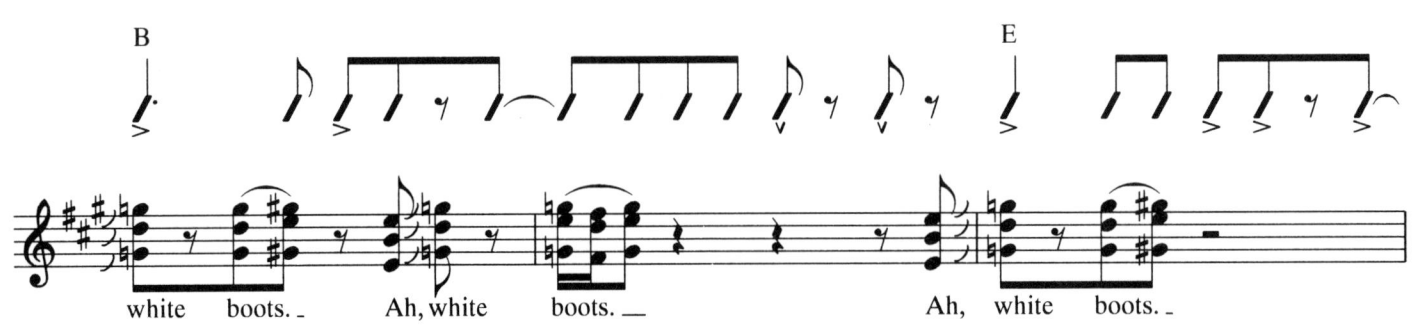

white boots. _ Ah, white boots. _ Ah, white boots. _

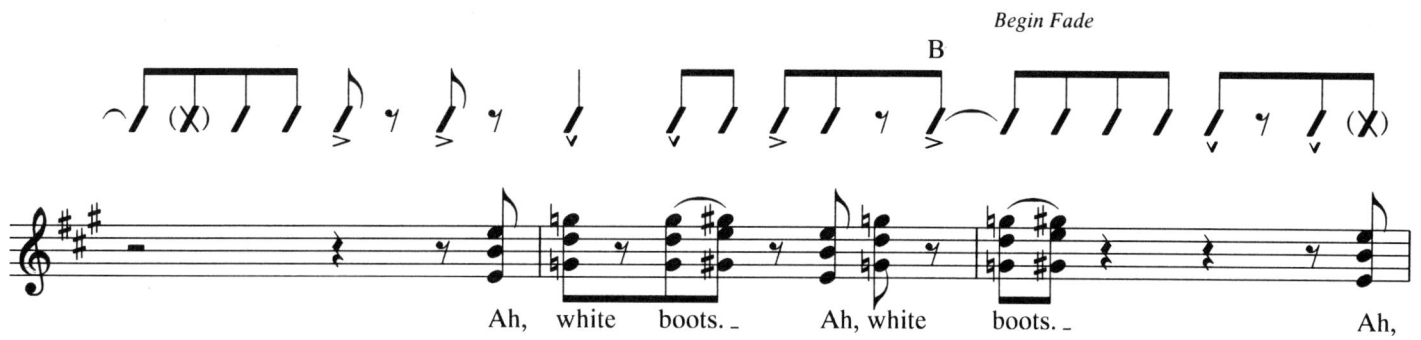

Ah, white boots. _ Ah, white boots. _ Ah,

white boots. ___ Ba - by in the

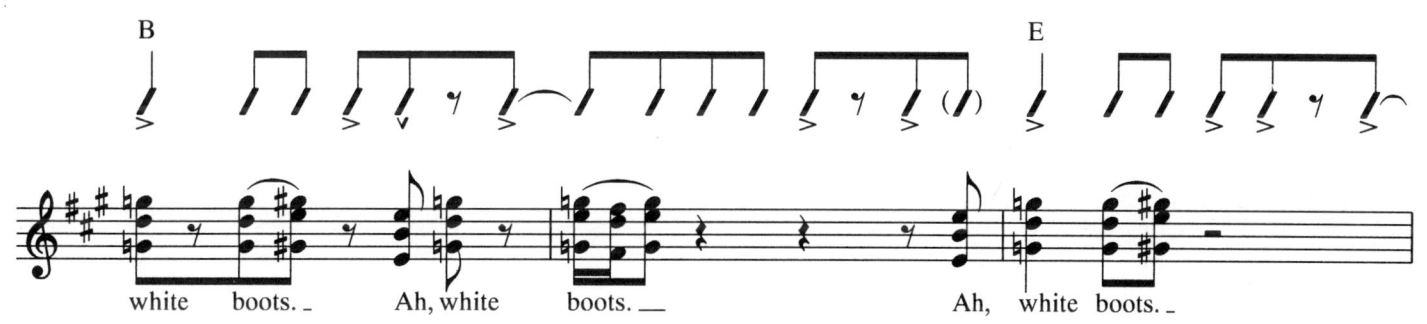

white boots. _ Ah, white boots. _ Ah, white boots. _

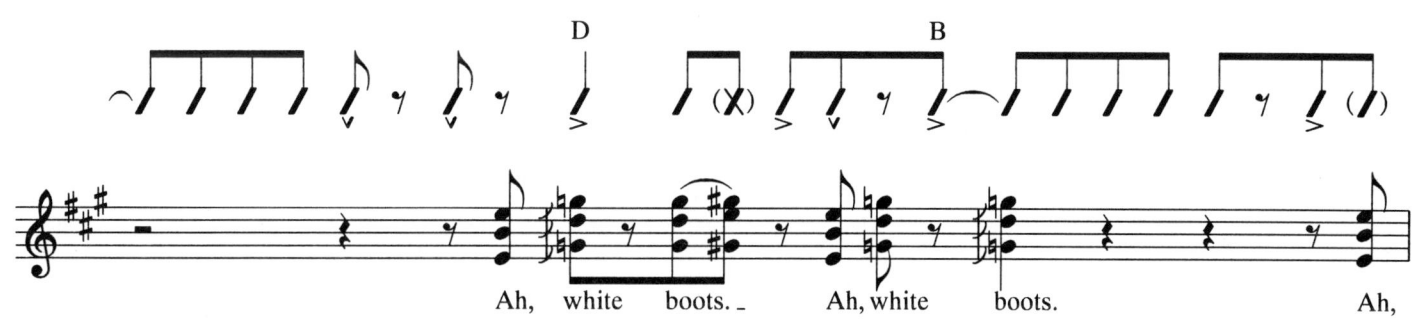

Ah, white boots. _ Ah, white boots. Ah,

white boots, ___ ah. _____ That's my ba - by (in the)

23

A smoking Texas-style instrumental, "D/FW" stands as a great example of the "less-is-more" school of composition.

Kicking off with a 2-bar single-note run (which is later refrained as the tag ending) no time is wasted stating the 24-bar melody; a classic blues phrase backed with a doubled bass figure. Sometimes laced with double-stops, this melody offers a blueprint of phrasing techniques for milking a simple blues lick for all it's worth.

B.B. King's phrasing comes to mind in the opening statement (bar 3), which contains three different slurs in one bar. Notice how each slur increases in speed and creates more tension. It's these little things that add up to more emotive, soulful playing.

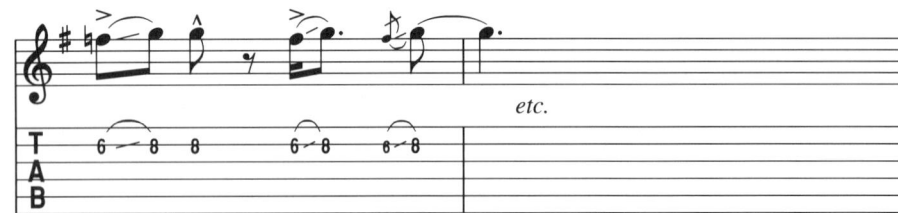

Try playing this bar without the slurs and note the lackluster difference.
The 2nd bar of melody (bar 4) used a frequently heard descending blues lick which you will see phrased two different ways throughout the tune:
Jimmie and Stevie Ray traded "fours" (4-bar phrases) throughout the melody on this one, and each man's style and phasing comes through loud and clear. The 2-bar figure that breaks up the melody phrases was actually recorded as a separate part but there's no reason not to play it between melodies to

or

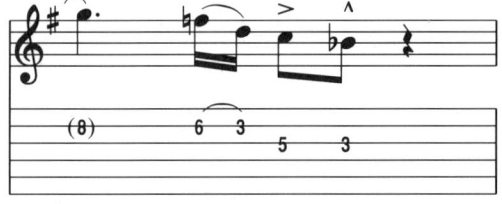

fill things out (especially if you're the only guitarist playing!)
A hammered grace note leads into the IV chord (C) melody lick before wrapping up with a variation of the tune's opening statement. To play this lick, station your fretting hand in the 6th position. (i.e., index finger at the 6th fret.) When you get to the C (1st string, 8th fret), reinforce your 3rd finger on the first string with your middle and index fingers at the 7th and 6th frets respectively. Then, push the string as if you were trying to scoop underneath it while still maintaining your grip. Practice slowly and be sure to bend to the proper pitch (you can check yourself against the 10th fret D note on the 1st string.) The same bend is played one octave lower in the repeated tag ending riff. The interlude lick in bar 59 (resembling Hendrix' "Hey Joe" intro) leads into a sustained low G that signals the return to the melody. Try adding vibrato to sustain the G for 5 bars.

More bending occurs in the second melody section at bar 33. To play this measure:

1. Station your hand in the 3rd position and play the 6th fret F with your 3rd finger.

2. Bend the F up a whole step <u>before</u> picking it (remember to use your middle and index fingers as back-ups) <u>then</u> pick it twice, release, re-bend and release all <u>without</u> re-picking the string.

Practice slowly and evenly and this technique will soon become a staple of your musical vocabulary.

D/FW

By Jimmie Vaughan

Spoken: "Howdy, folks! Welcome to D/FW!"

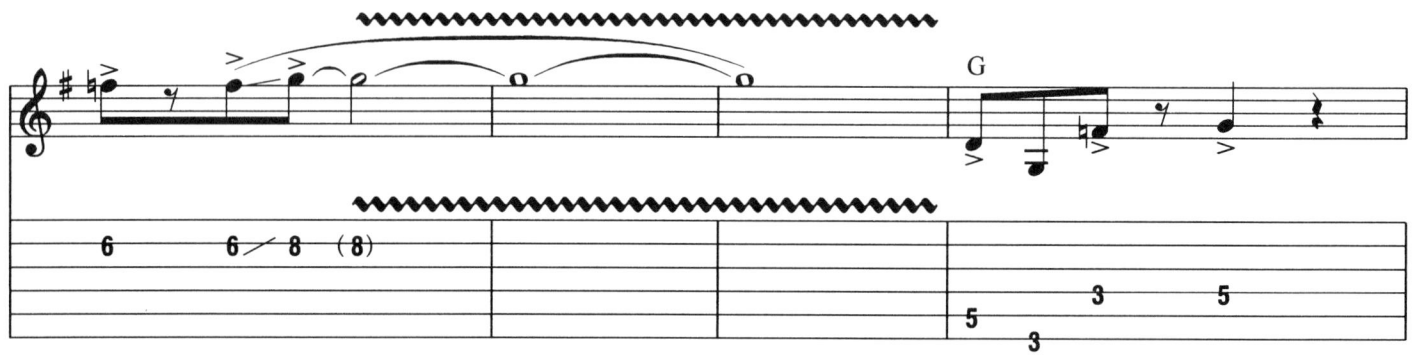

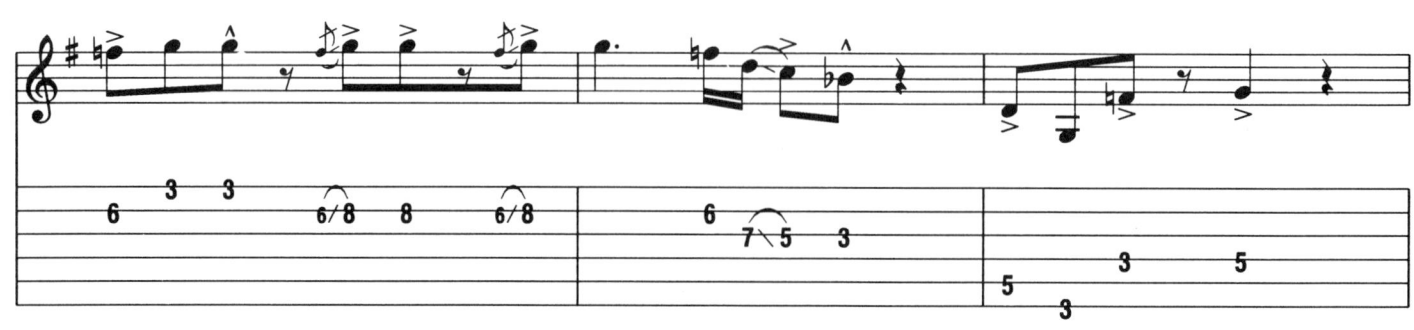

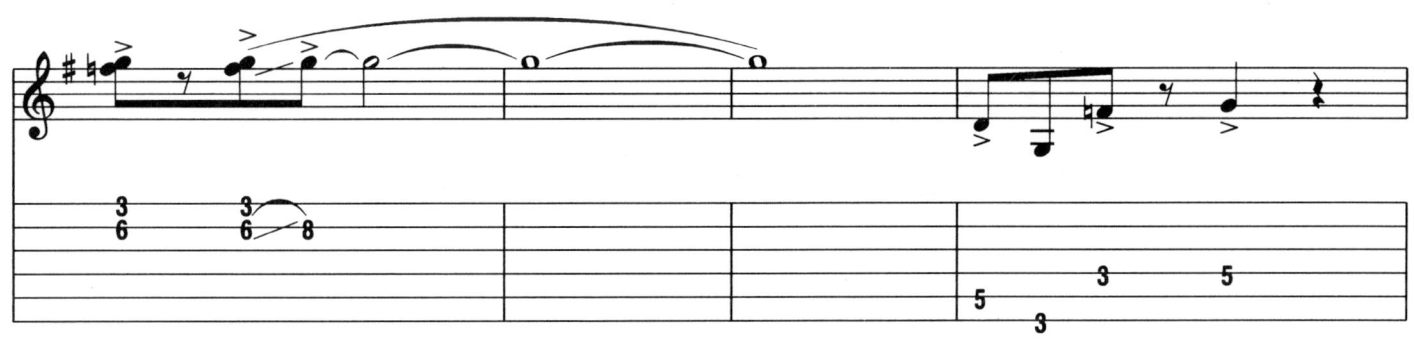

Guitar Solo

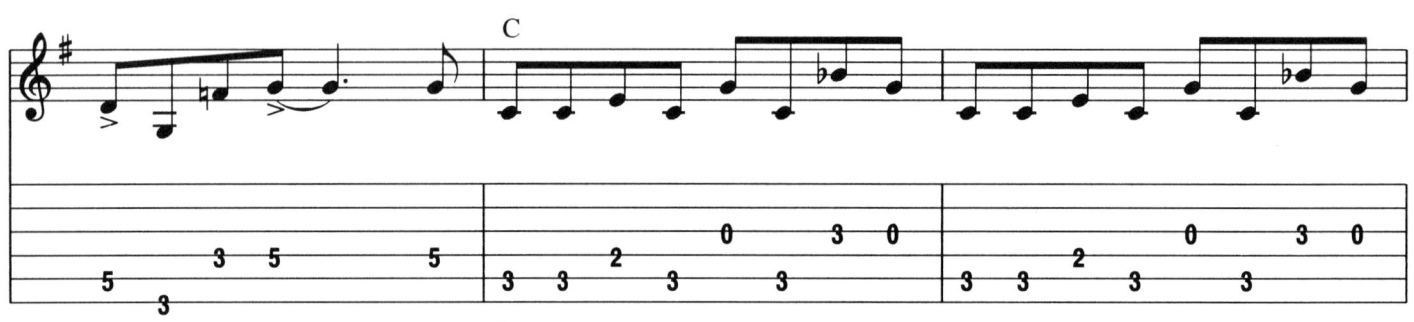

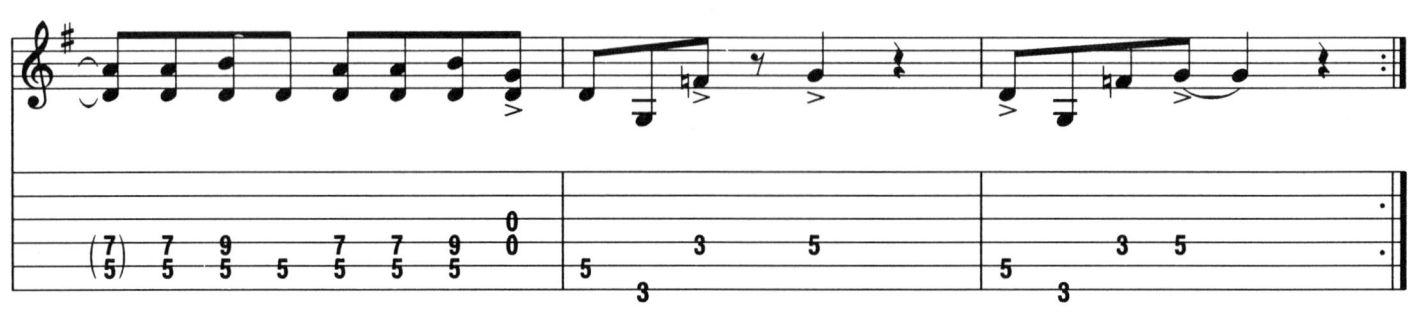

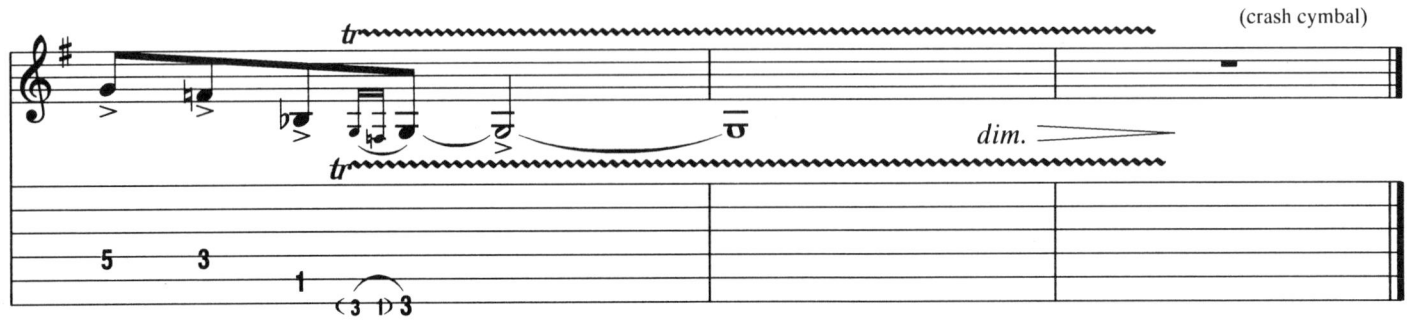

GOOD TEXAN

LESSON

The sound of muted, low-pitched guitar strings has conjured musical visions of the old West from "Happy Trails" to "The Wild, Wild West." The insistent rhythm guitar figure from "Good Texan" not only provides a healthy dose of western swing but offers more valuable insights on the technique of palm-muting.

Built from just three notes in the 5th position, this clicky line lays the foundation for much of the tune. The eighth notes are played as "swing-eighth's" throughout. That is, on the first and last beats of the eighth note triplets built from each quarter note. Lay the butt of your picking palm lightly against the strings where they pass over the bridge saddles. The amount of palm pressure controls the amount of muting that occurs. If your vibrato tailpiece is set to float (pull up as well as drop down) you must be careful not to exert pressure on the bridge, as this will put you out of tune as you play.

A slightly busier variation of the figure is heard during the call and response format in the Verses. The switch to the IV chord (A) is fleshed out with a boogie-woogie-type bass movement built around an open position A chord.

The 2/4 bar at the end of the Chorus turns the Intro rhythm figure around backwards before another 2/4 bar reverts it for the next verse. You may also try counting this section straight through in 4/4.

The 2nd and 3rd verses feature some double-stop punctuations in response to the vocals. Try interspersing these fills with the rhythm figure.

The Outro contains a few variations such as the microtonal 1/4 step bend punctuations in bar 83. Play these smoothly, being careful not to overbend. Adding 1/4 step bends is yet another subtle phrasing technique that can breathe new life into your lines.

Good Texan

By Jimmie Vaughan and Nile Rodgers

E5

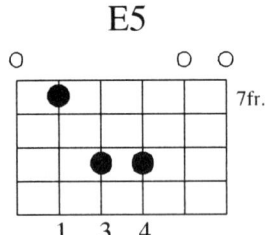

B5

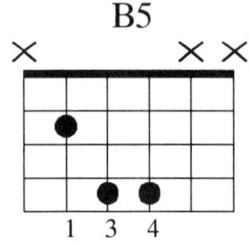

D5

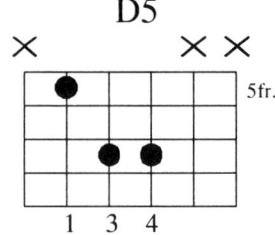

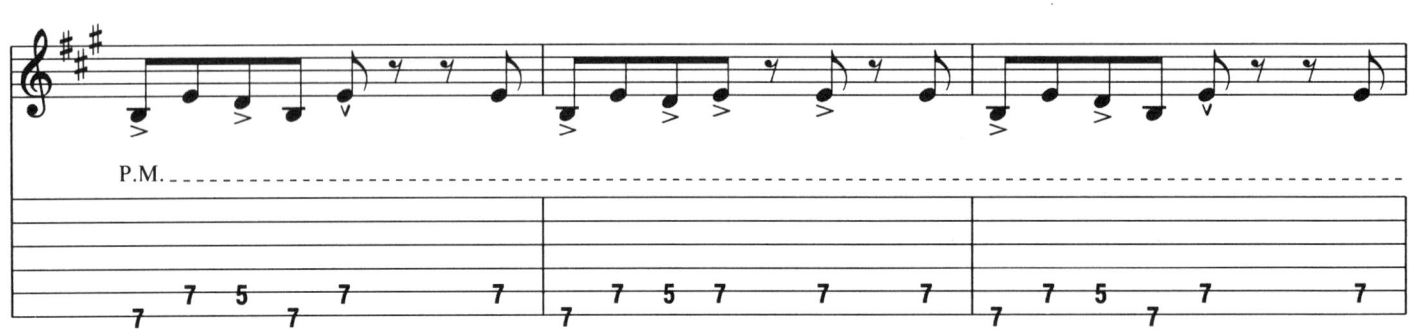

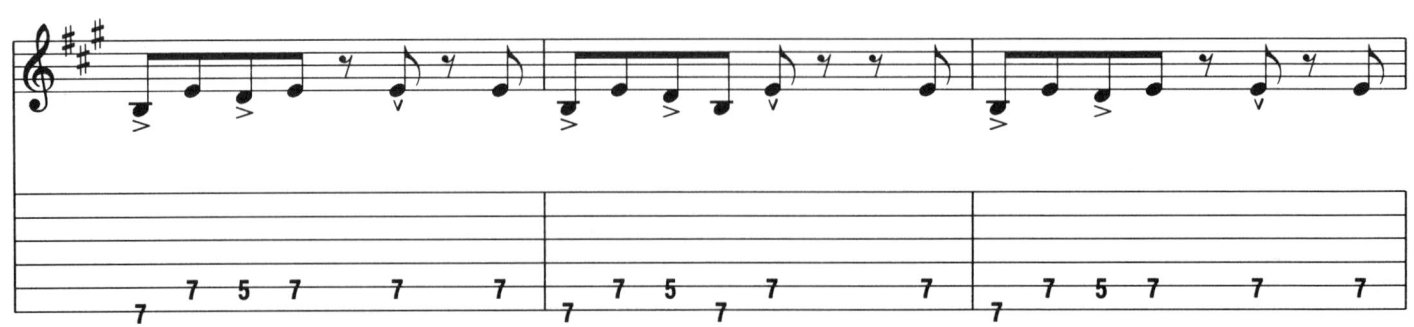

Verse

(E5)

1. Say things __ to __ me like a cow-girl __ would. __

I'll do tricks for __ ya like a cow-boy - should. __

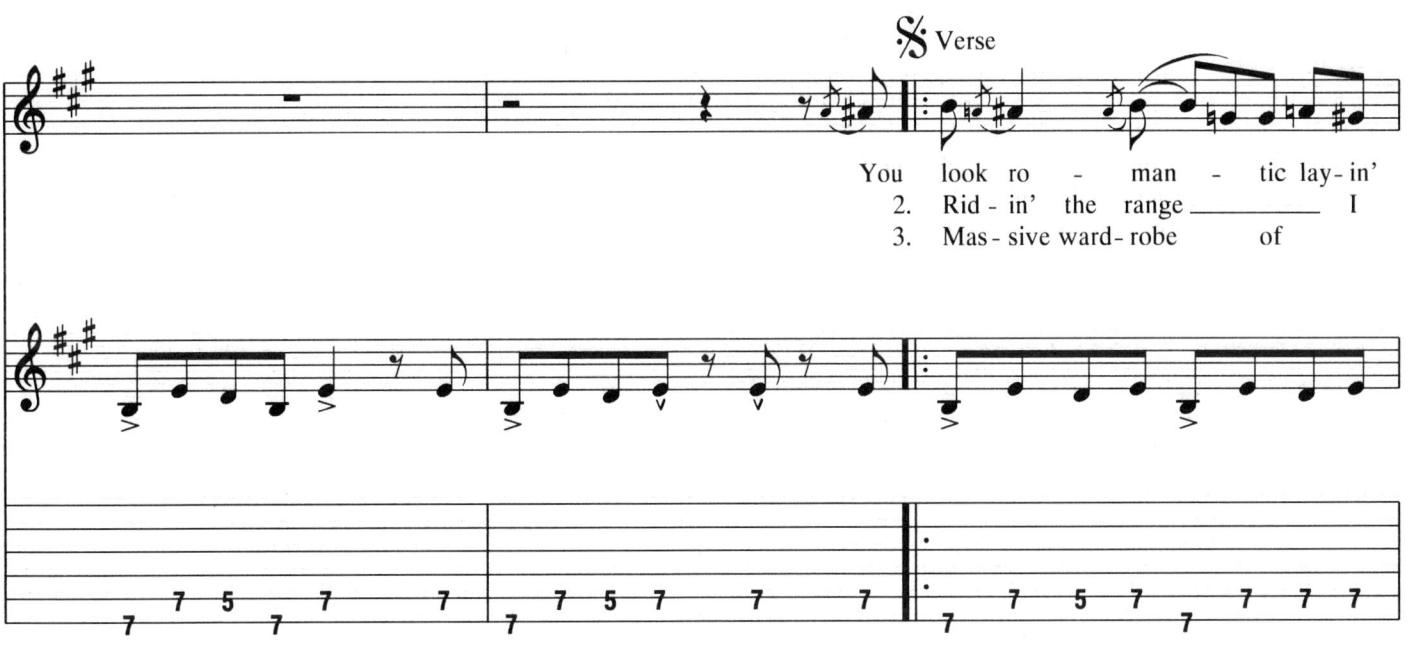

Verse

You look ro - man - tic lay - in'
2. Rid - in' the range _____ I
3. Mas - sive ward-robe of

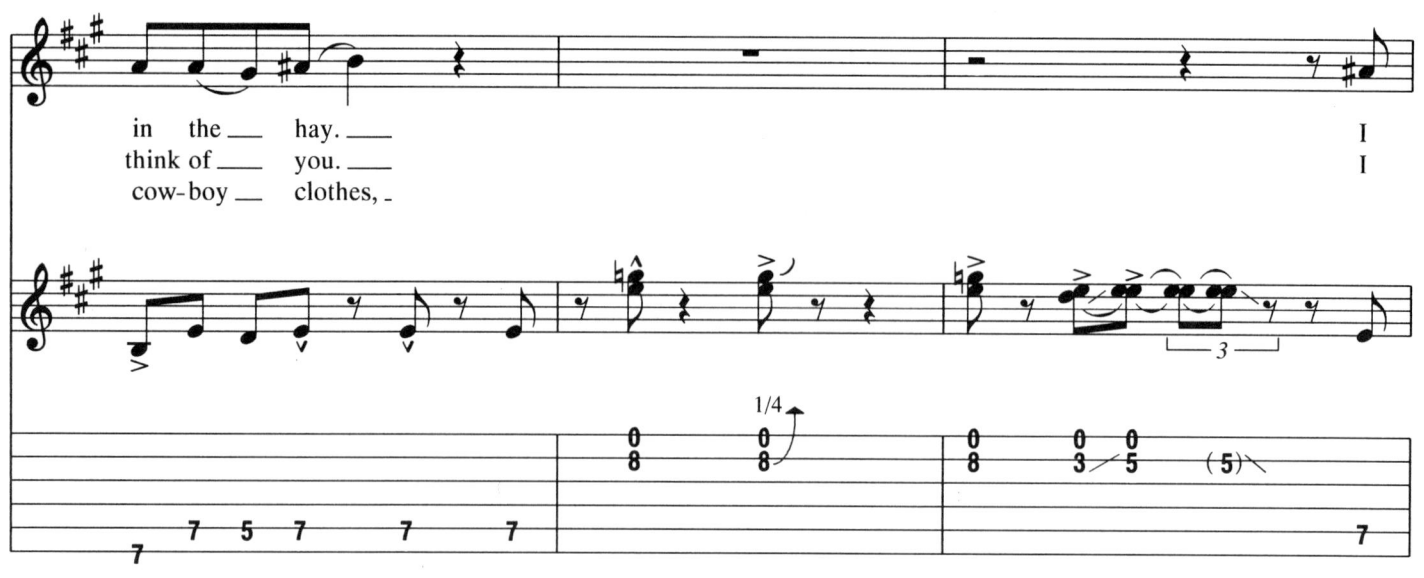

in the ___ hay. ___
think of ___ you. ___
cow-boy ___ clothes, __

need ya to-night __ in a new kind of way. __
dig your chil-i, you know it's true. _____
top of my head to the tip of my toes. __

Cue notes: 2nd & 3rd verses

When __ ya look at - me, ___ ah, with those __ eyes, _____
Aw, I make big mon-ey, put it in the bank. _____
Aw, you look so good in my hat with fringe on it.

2nd & 3rd verses

it makes me start __ to fan -
That long-horn Cad-dy's got a
So put on my boots mmm,__

- ta - size. ____
great big tank. ____
dog-gone it. ____

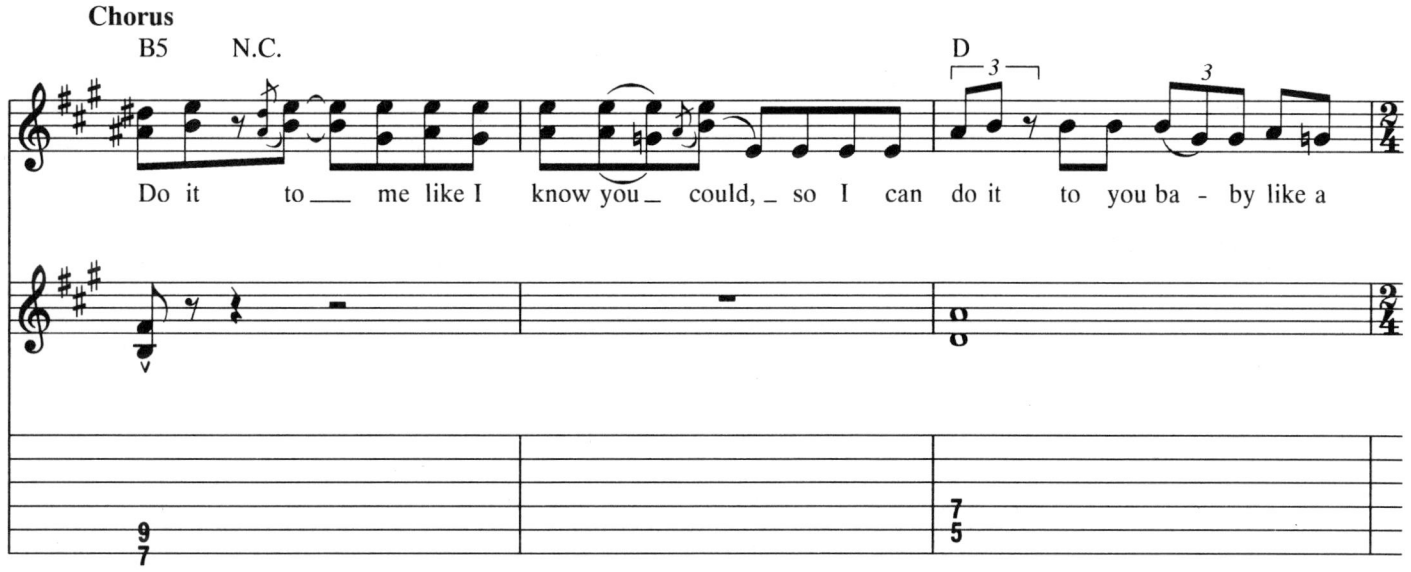

Chorus

Do it to __ me like I know you __ could, __ so I can do it to you ba - by like a

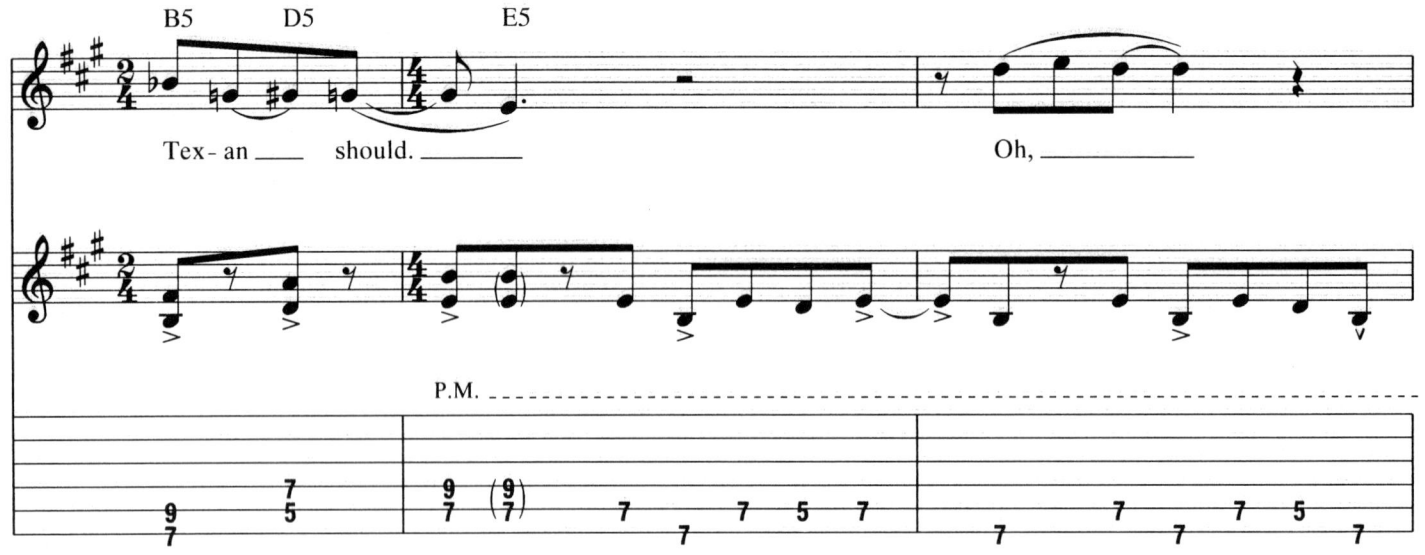

Tex-an ____ should. ____ Oh, _____

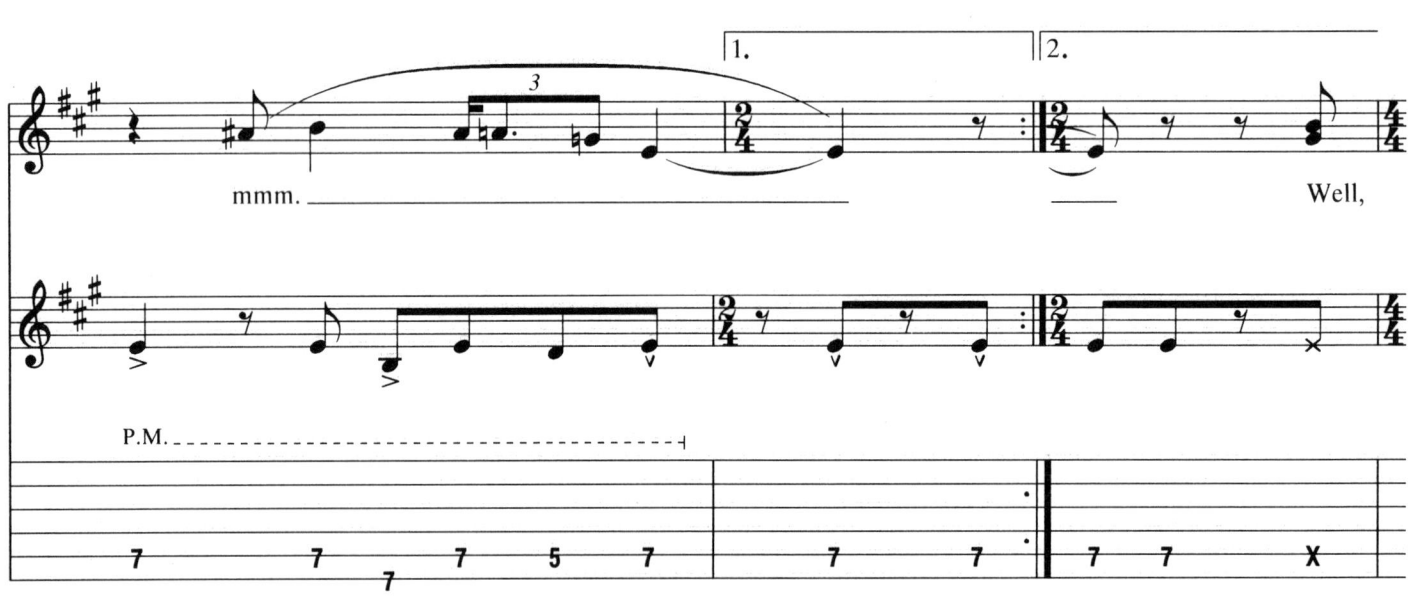

mmm. _____ 1. 2. Well,

Bridge

you're the kind-a wom-an who's a-bove the ____ rest. ____ Well,

Guitar Solo

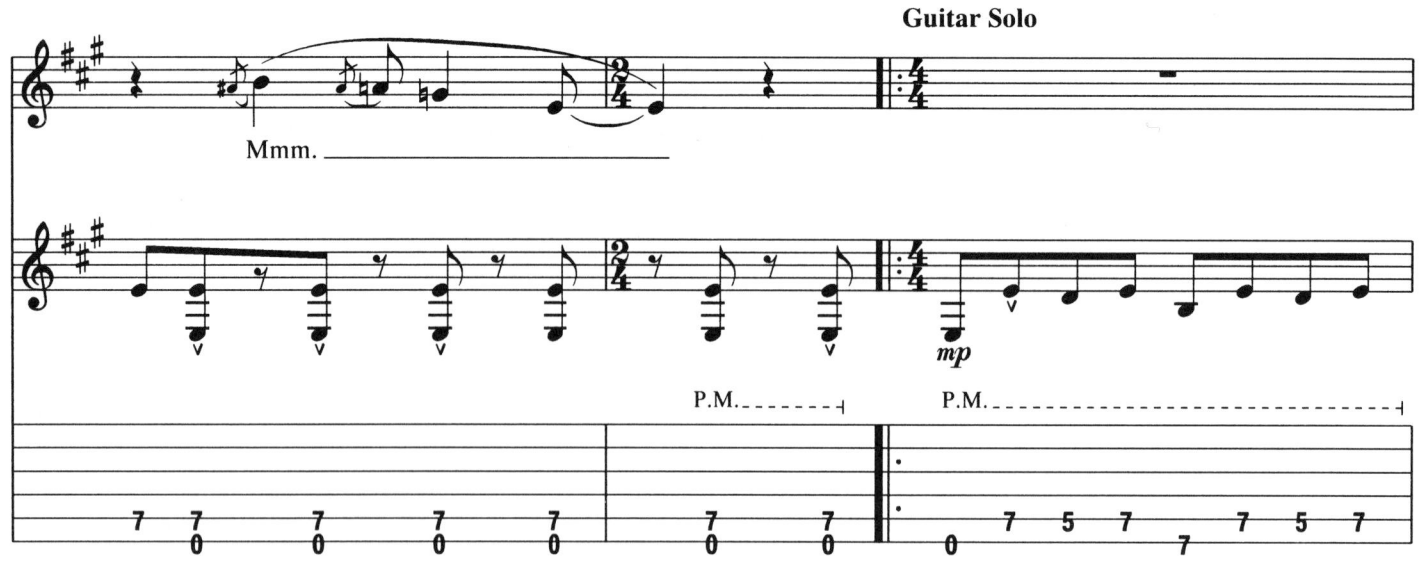

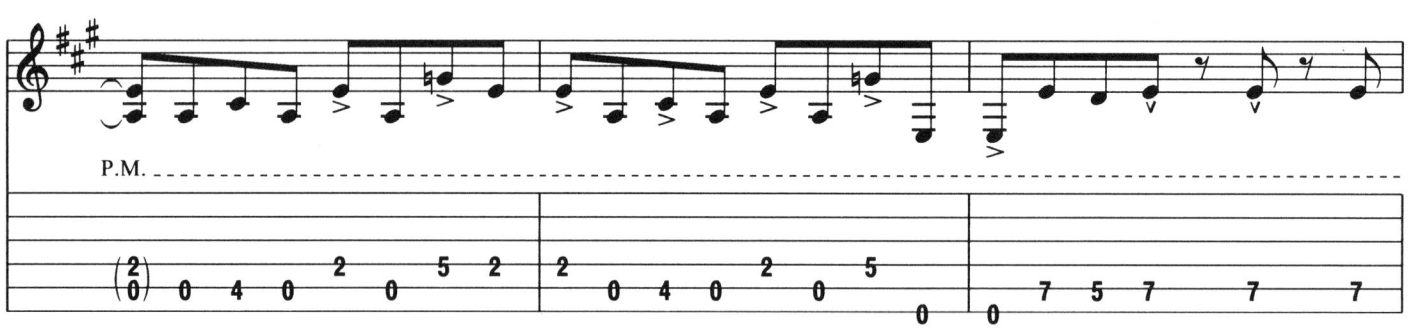

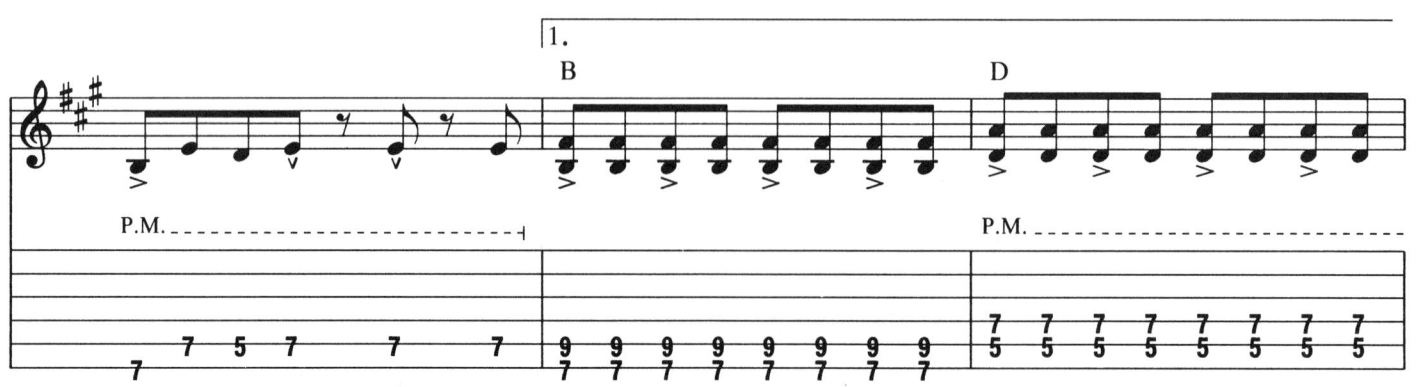

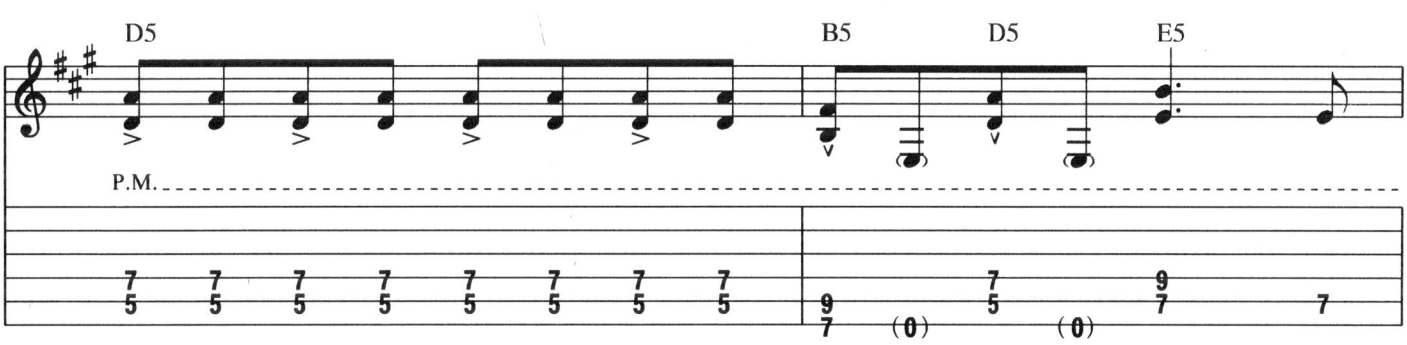

D.S. al Coda

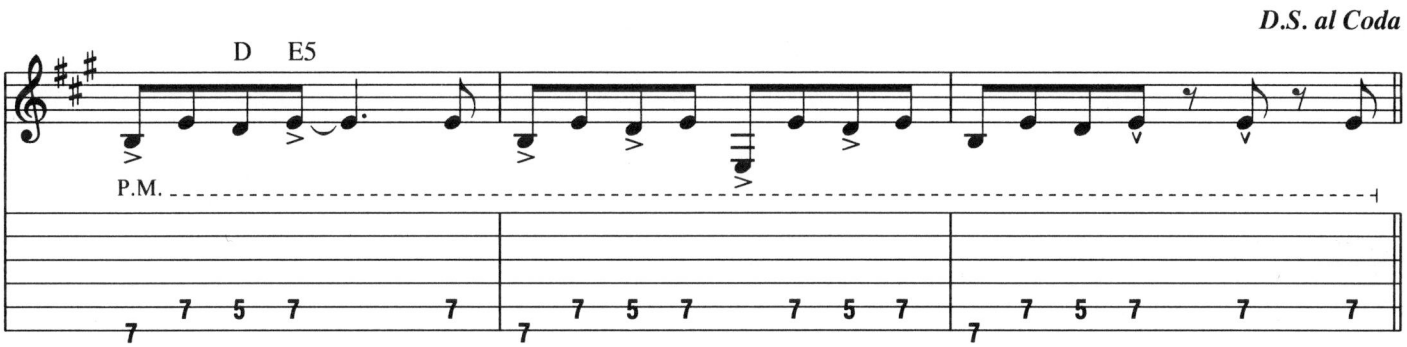

⊕ *Coda*

Chorus

Do it to ____ me like I know you ____ could. ____ I'll

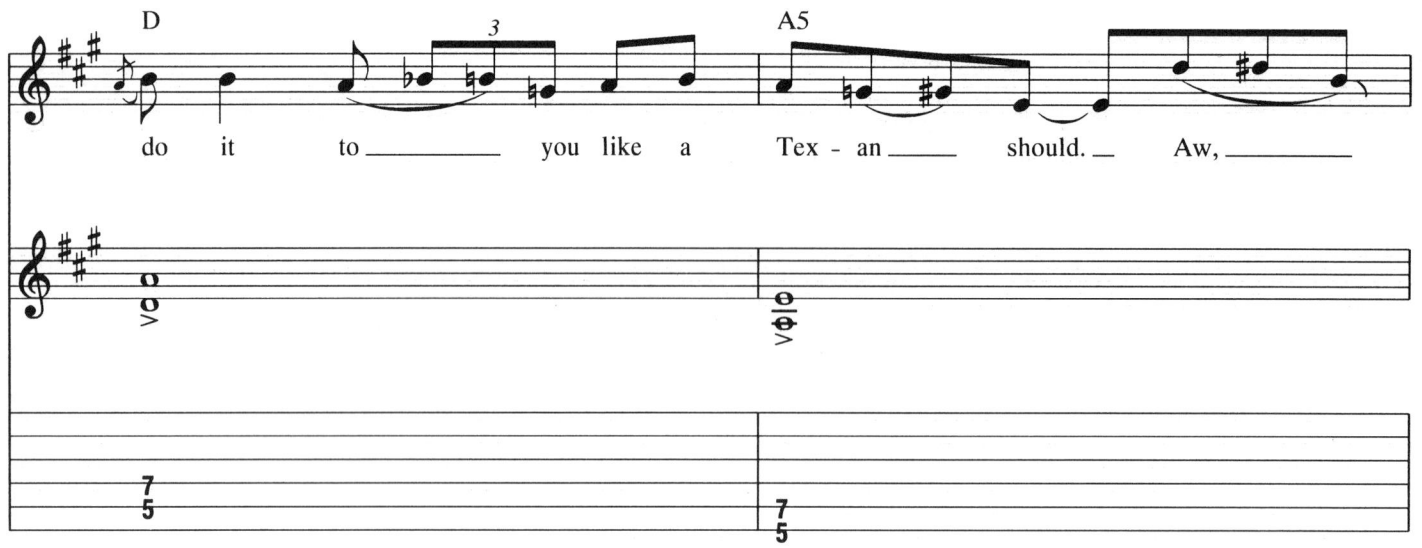

do it to _____ you like a Tex - an _____ should. ___ Aw, _____

do ____ it to me ba - by like I know __ you ____ could, ___ so I can

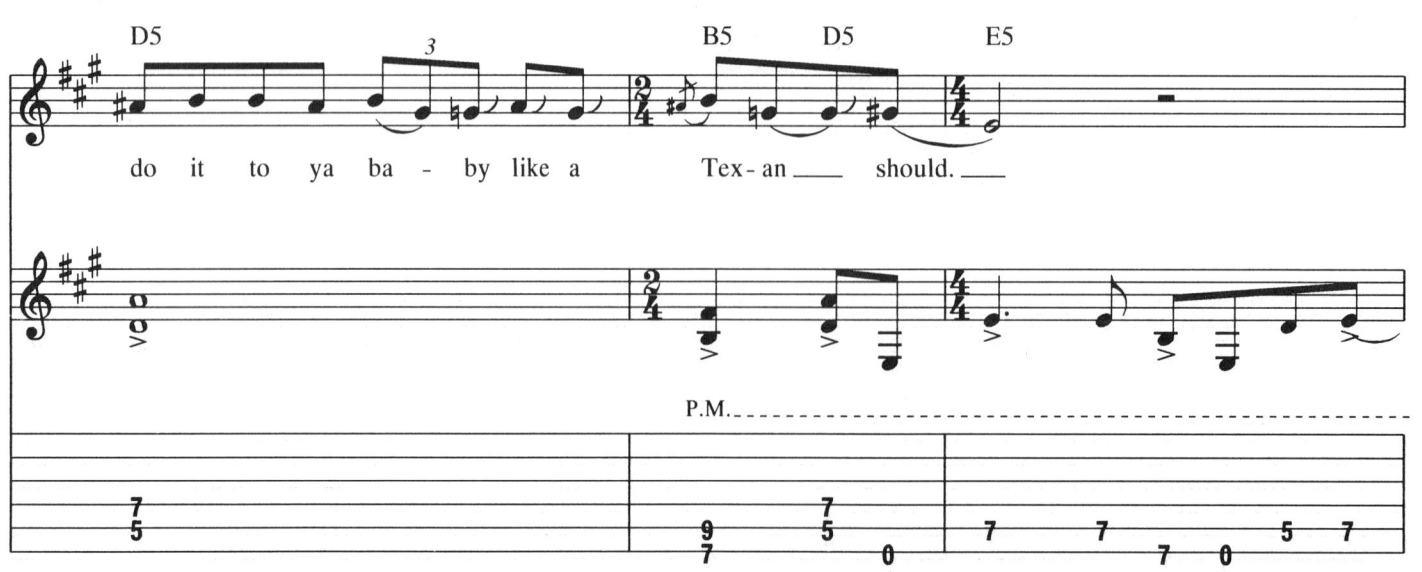

do it to ya ba - by like a Tex - an _____ should. ___

P.M.----------------

Oh, _____ mmm. _____

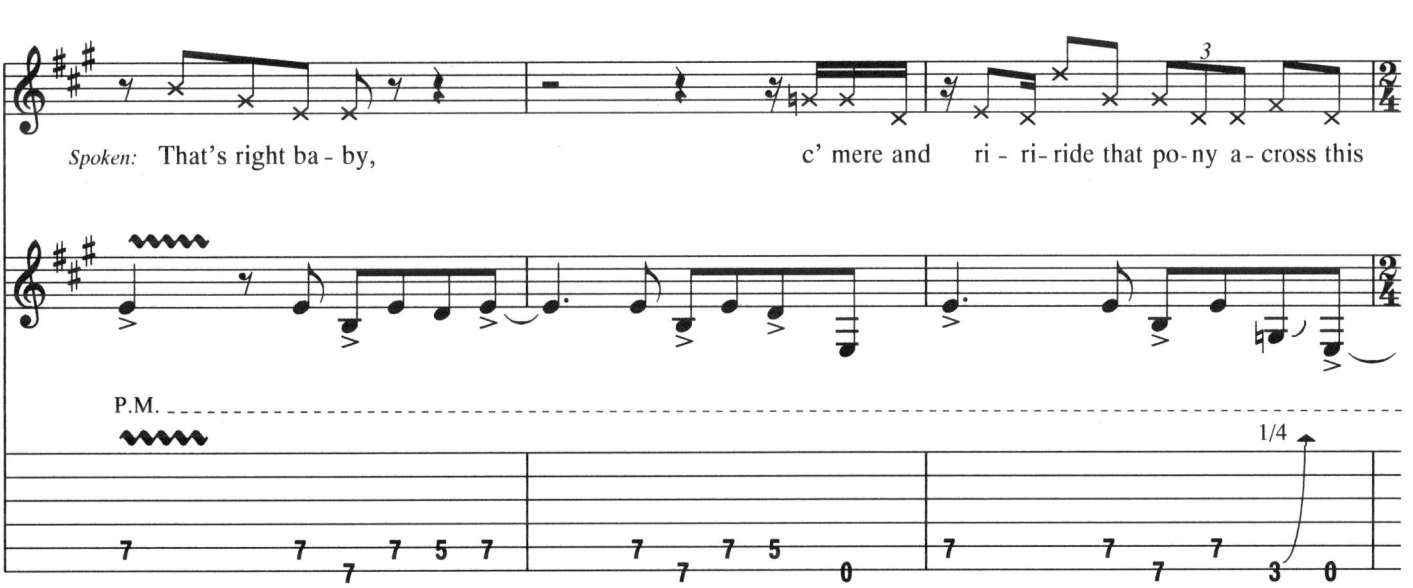

Spoken: That's right ba - by, c' mere and ri - ri - ride that po - ny a - cross this

bridge! You're a good _

lit - tle part-ner!

That's right ba-by, come on.

You know there ain't but one man __ for you, __ and that's me.

Like a good Tex-an should.

I love it! (Heh, heh.) That's __ it! That's __ it! Woo! __

HILLBILLIES FROM OUTERSPACE

LESSON

Jimmie Vaughan originally played the melody and solos on "Hillbillies From Outer Space" on an 8-string steel guitar tuned down 1/2 step (E♭ – C♭ - A♭ - G♭ - E♭ - C♭ - B♭♭ - C♭ for the curious). The whole deal is arranged for standard 6-string tuned down 1/2 step. You can switch on a moderately fast flange or chorus to help simulate Jimmie Vaughan's organ-like tone on the recording. This is the first 12 bar blues of the bunch, which of course refers to the following progression:

| I chord |✗|✗|✗| IV chord |✗| I chord |✗| V | IV | I |✗|

Again, thinking of the melody fragments as moveable shapes can speed the learning process. Begin by learning the 7th position V chord (B) lick in the Intro. (The notes outline B minor 7th.) Notice that moving the lick down a whole step to the 5th position and raising the second note 1/2 step is all that's necessary to adapt the lick to the IV chord (A) when adding grace notes, be sure to accent the hammered note playing the grace note as quickly as possible. The I chord (E) lick is a blues staple covered by everyone from
John Lee Hooker to Eric Clapton.

To get a steel-like ring to the melody, strive to execute all hammer-ons cleanly (notice that the hammers occur in time in the melody; be careful not to rush them as grace notes). Let the notes that form chord shapes ring together. You might even be tempted to try hybrid picking on this one. That is, using the pick in conjuction with your middle finger. Try this lick both ways.

The 3rd Chorus (each cycle of a 12-bar blues progression is called a <u>chorus</u>) melody begins in the 5th position, outlining E before shifting to the 10th position over A . The 7th position B and 5th position A licks are also identical.

The 6th chords in the Solo are tasty and will come in handy in many other 12-bar blues situations. The arrangement switches to Stevie Ray Vaughan's rhythm part during Jimmie Vaughan's solo steel choruses. Witness the effective use of palm-muting giving the part a real "lowdown" feel and allowing Steve Ray Vaughan's frequent accents to speak out. Also of note are Stevie Ray Vaughan's accents on beats 2 and 4 throughout.

The melodies from bar 70 on are played in two different octaves and are interspersed with 6th chords. If you've heard the E6/9 voicing at the end (perhaps in Hendrix' "Third Stone From The Sun" or Stevie Ray Vaughan's "Lenny"), but never played it, memorize, adopt, and savor its unique flavor. It may be the ultimate pleasure chord!

Hillbillies From Outerspace

By Jimmie Vaughan and Stevie Ray Vaughan

8 String Steel Gtr. Arr. for 6 String
Tune Down 1/2 Step

④=D♭ ①=E♭
⑤=A♭ ②=B♭
⑥=E♭ ③=G♭

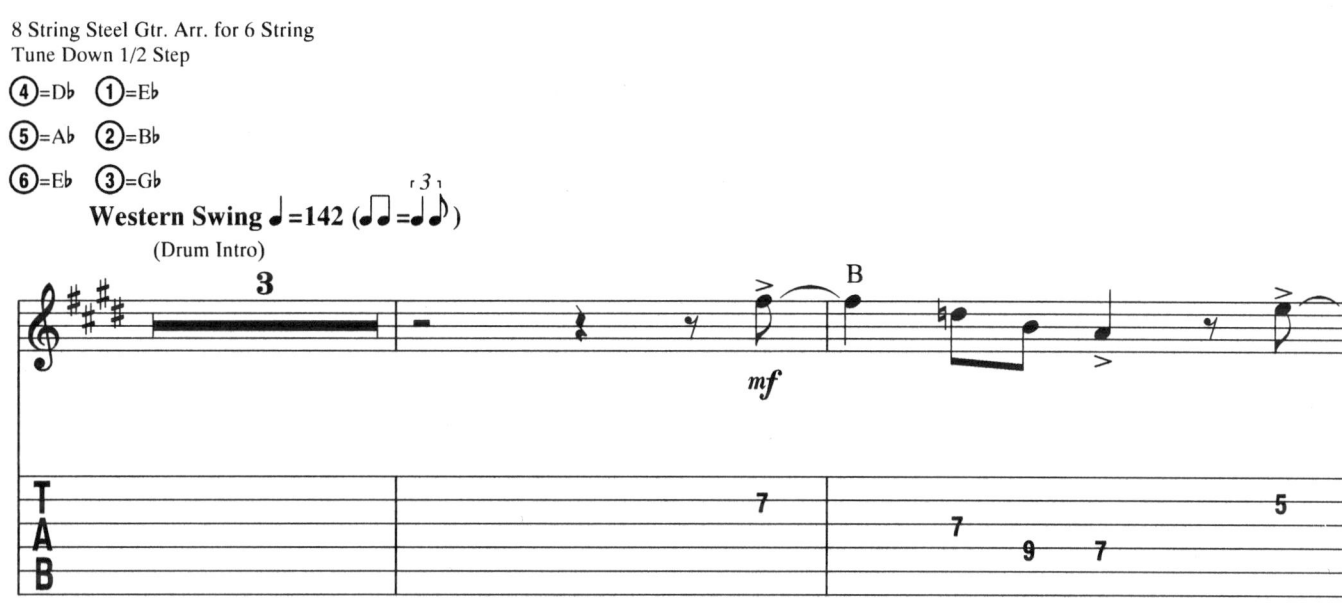

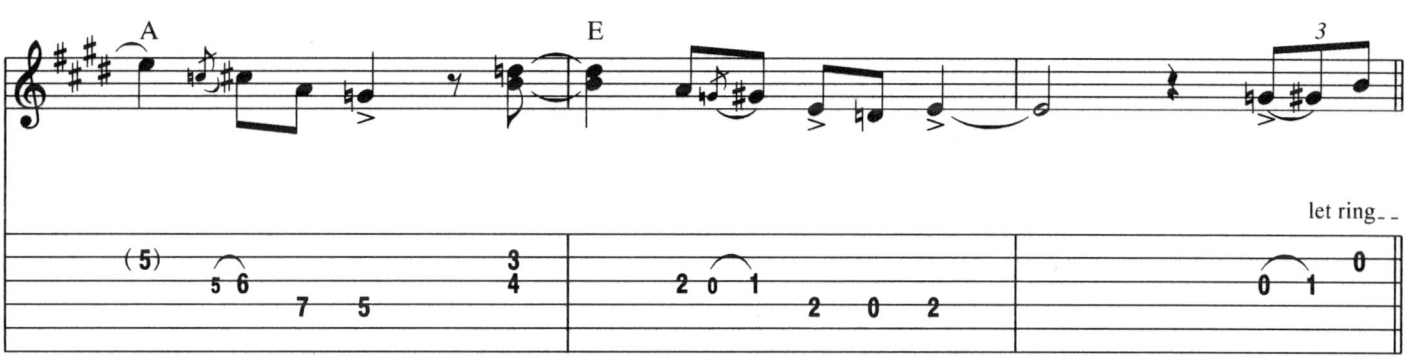

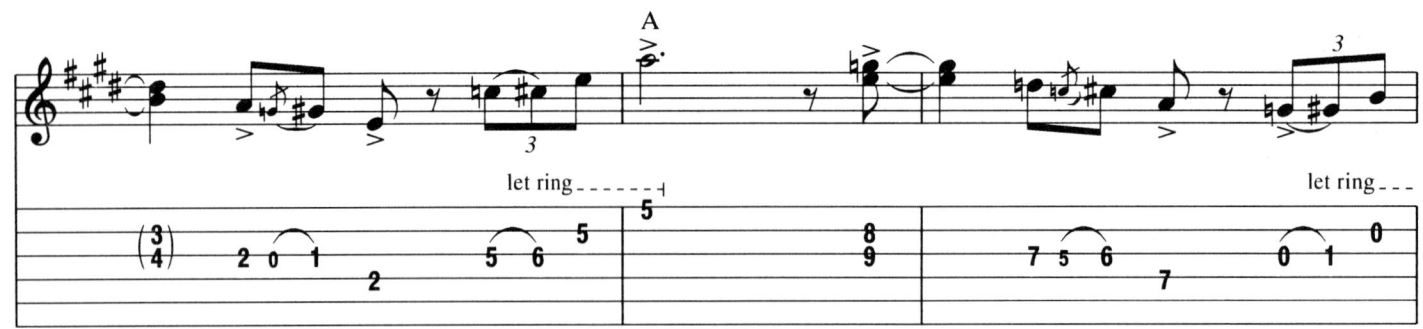

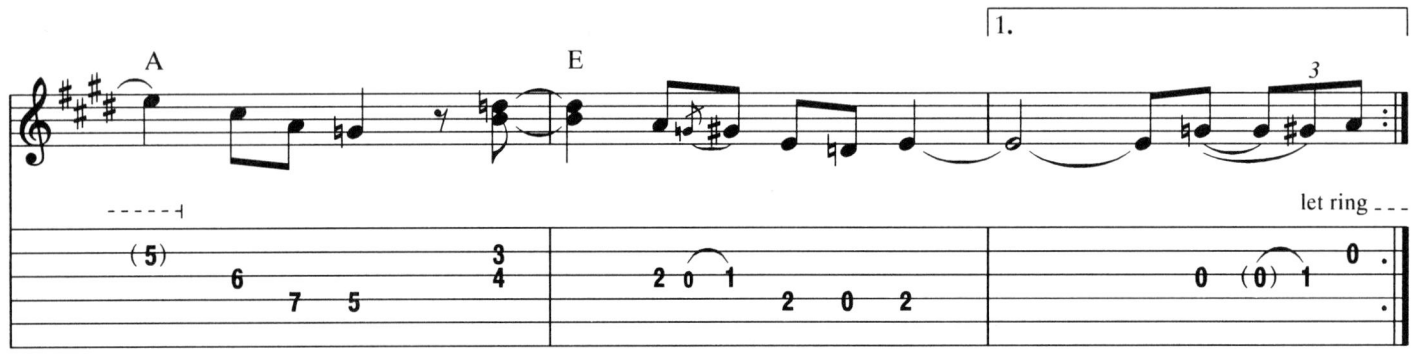

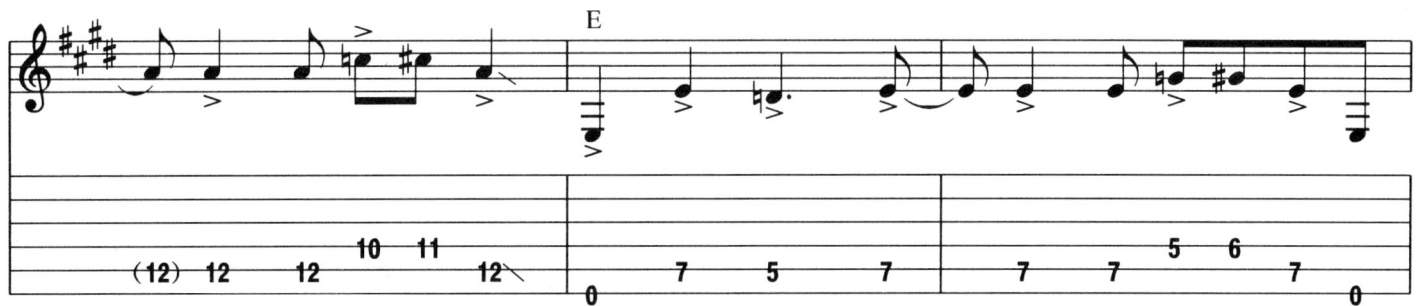

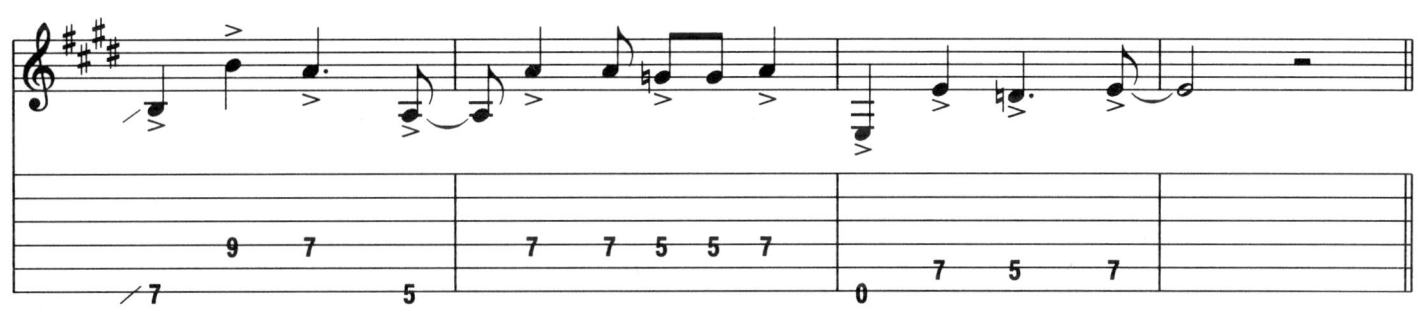

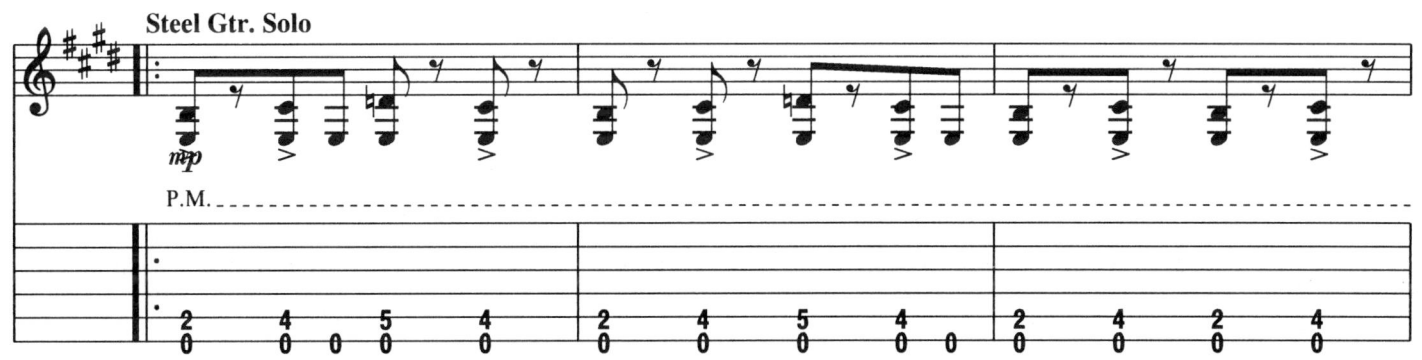

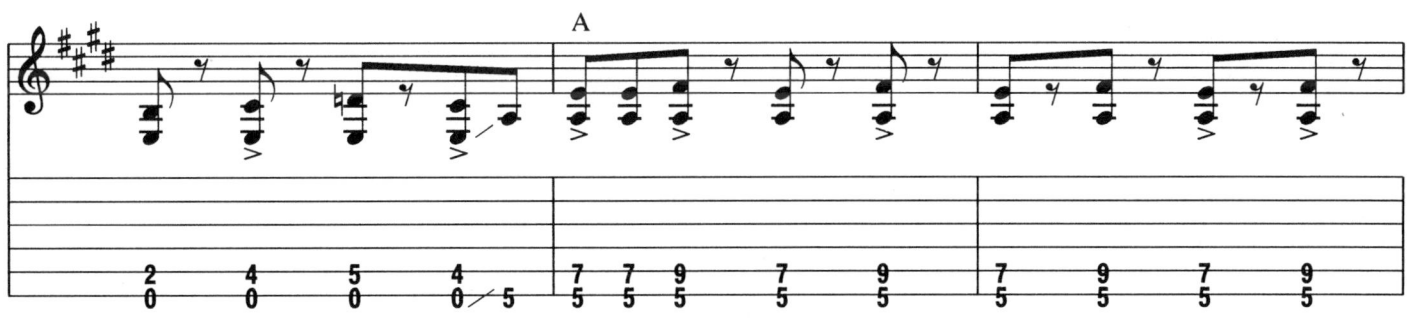

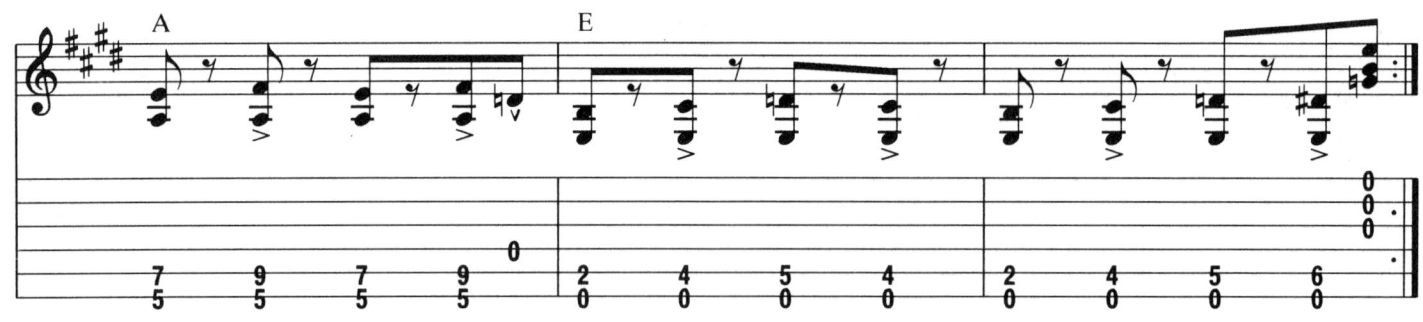

8 String Steel Gtr. Arr. for 6 String

Guitar Solo

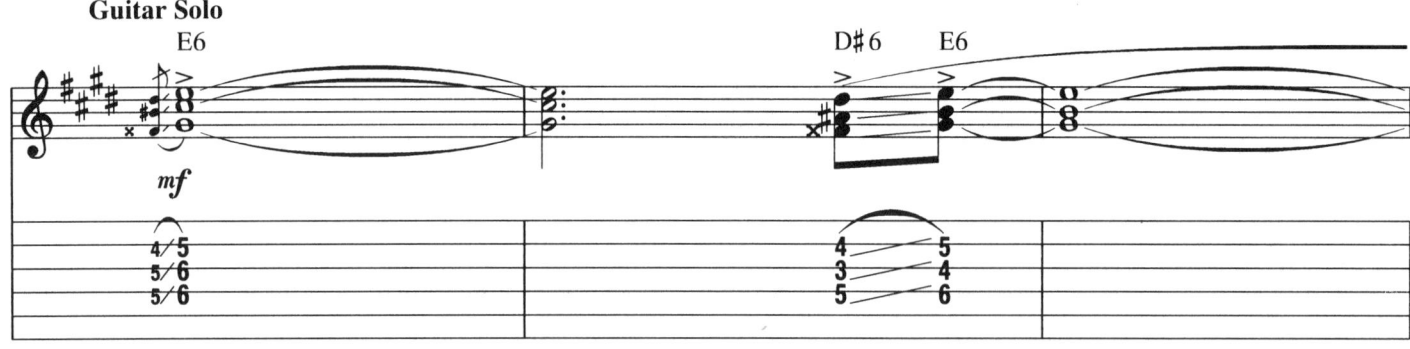

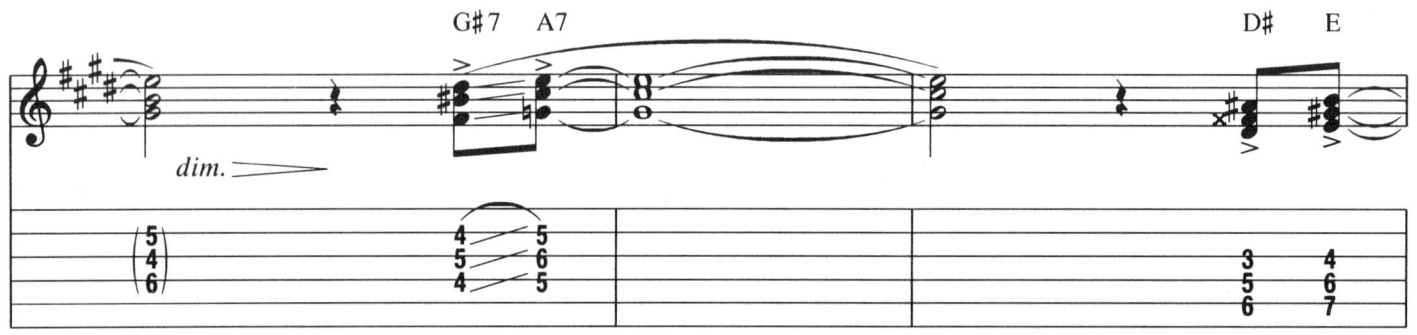

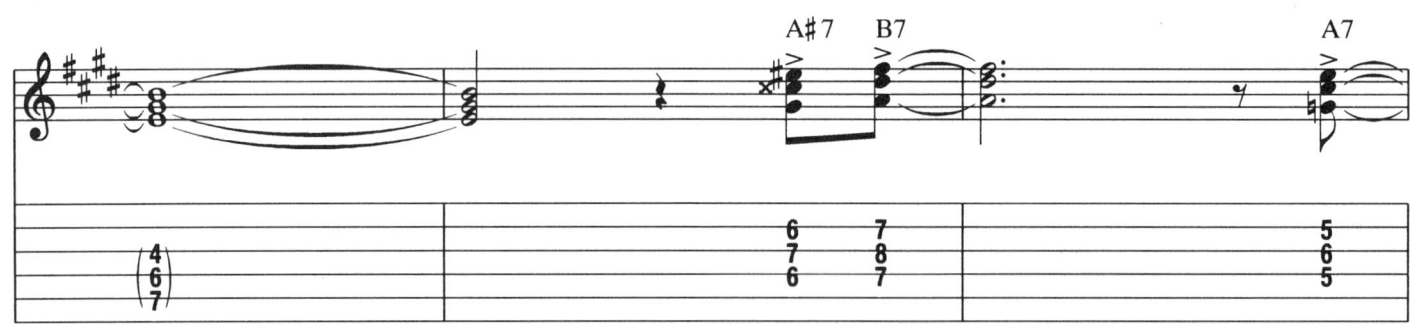

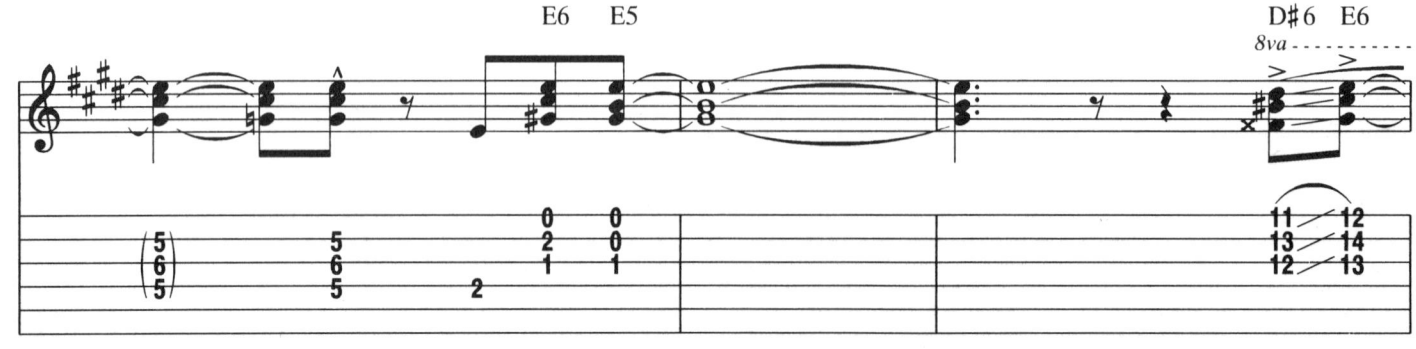

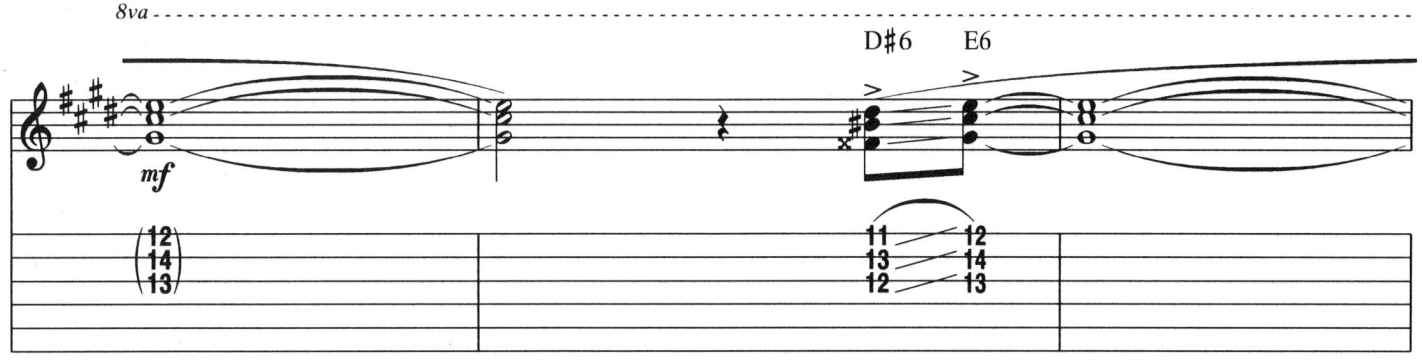
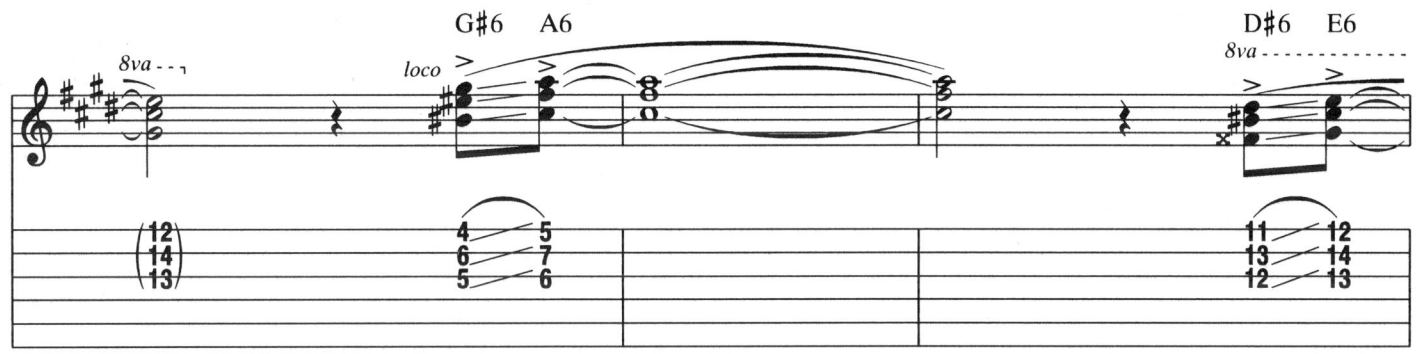
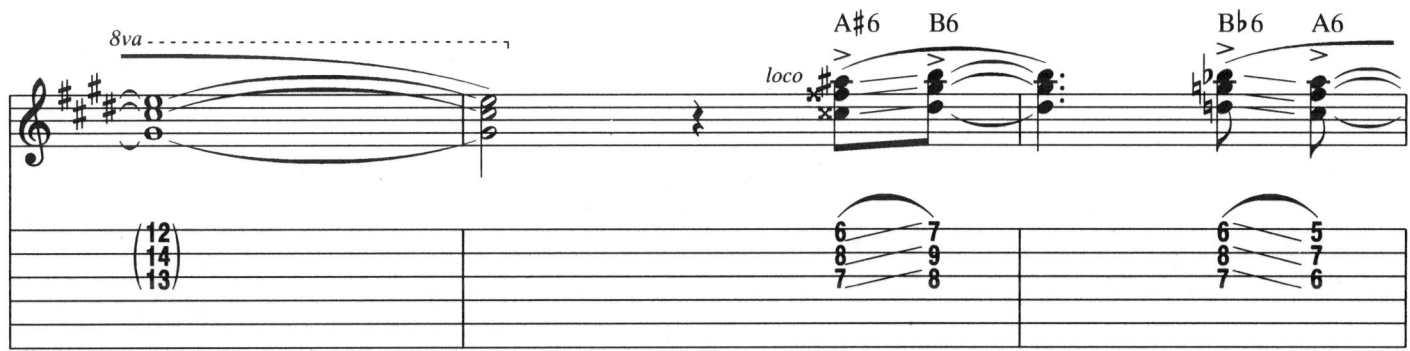
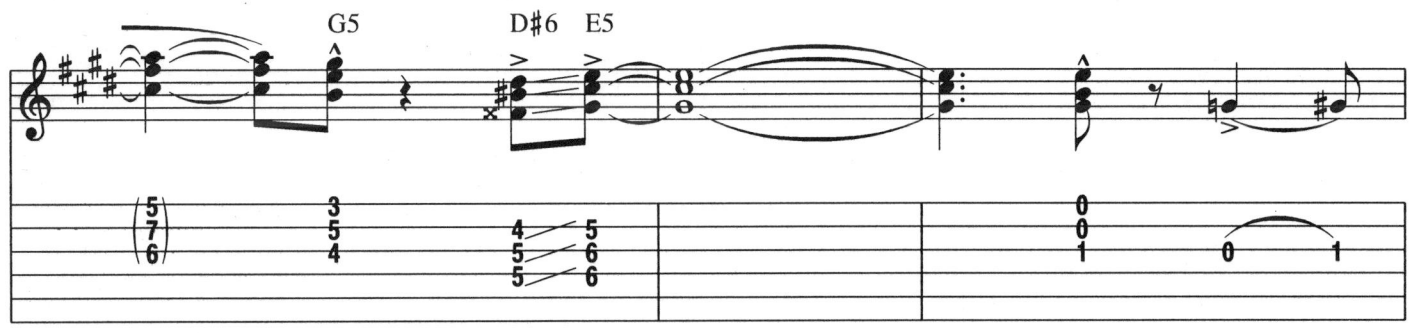

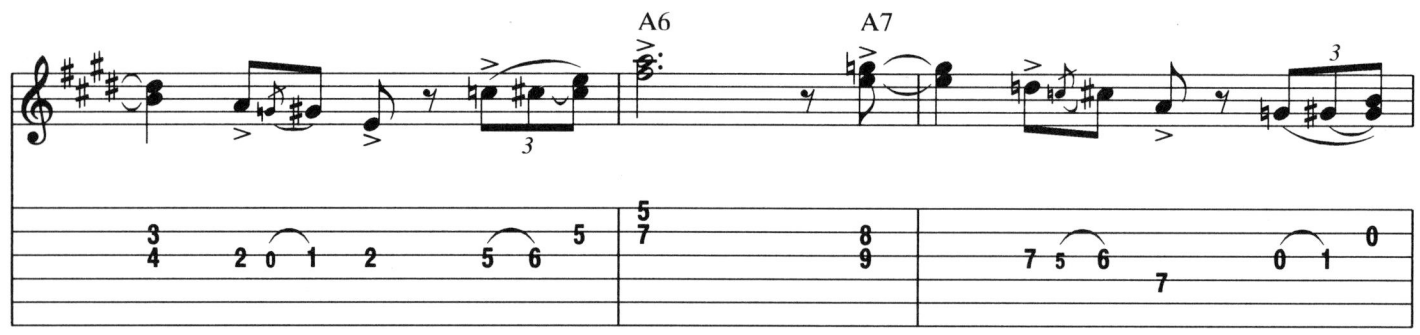

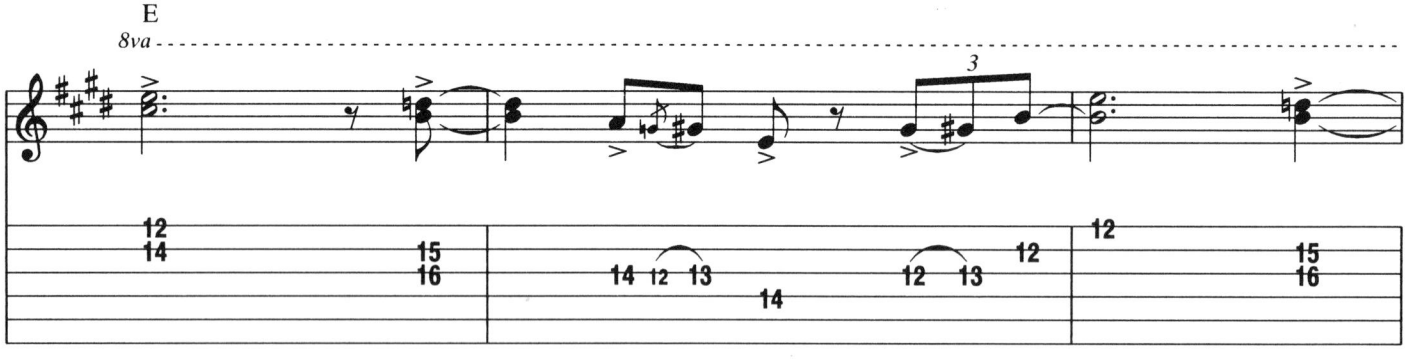

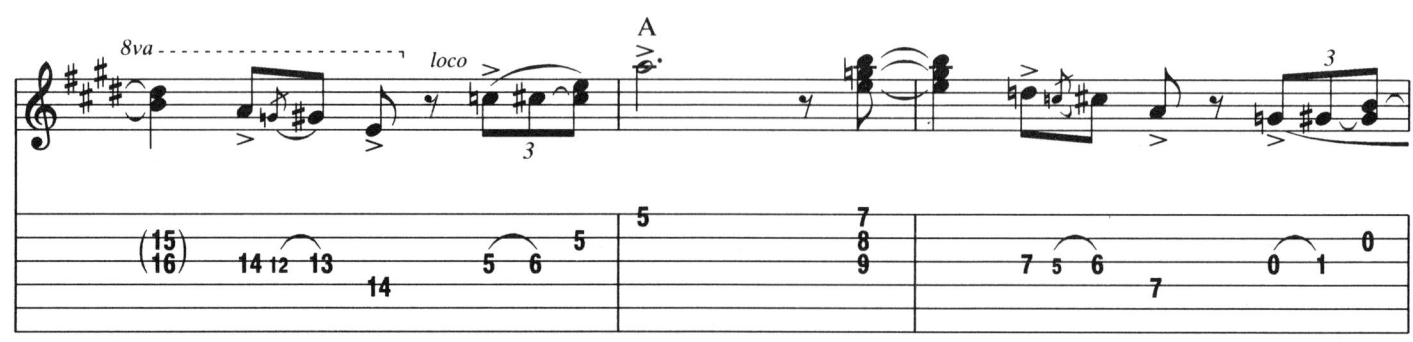

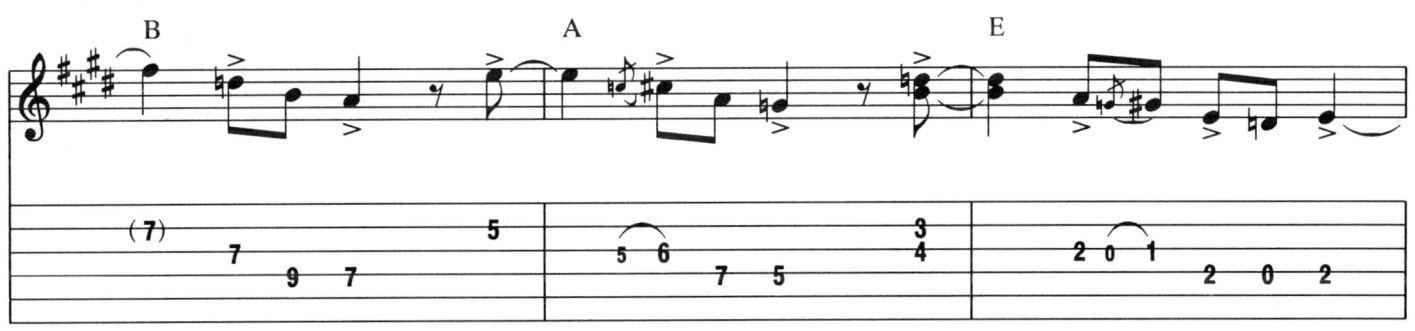

LONG WAY FROM HOME

LESSON

Especially evident in "Long Way From Home" is the effect of tuning down 1/2 step: the main E chord rhythm figure (first heard in bar 10) exudes a larger-than-life quality. This is because the chord is actually an E♭ voicing not possible in standard tuning.

The Intro riff again involves a series of moveable shapes beginning in the 7th position. Notice how the lick outlines the tonic octave B's on the 6th and 4th strings. Visualizing these "target points" will make position shifts easier.

Start by picking every note (adding the hammer-ons later) and make a repetitive exercise out of the first 2 bars. Keep your alternate picking consistent with the eighth note pulse. Muted beats (x) may consist of one or more muted strings. The muting action occurs by releasing pressure with the fretting hand while still maintaining contact points. These muted accents also facilitate easier chord changing, buying precious fractions of seconds. Guitarists can even assume a percussive role in the rhythm section while keeping their time together in this manner. Try inserting muted accents wherever rests occur in this figure and check out how funky you can get!

Once you've got this lick wired in the 7th position over B^7, simply move it down to the 5th position for A, 3rd position for G, and so on. Note how on the F# and F changes, the figure doubles up to get us back to the "target" E figure on time.

The grace note in the figure hammers the flat 3rd to the 3rd in typical blues fashion. Again, count time with alternate pickstrokes, playing downbeats with downstrokes and upbeats with upstrokes. Some Verse figure chords are in the open position while some are moveable shapes. Note how the root is often played alone, anticipating the chord at different points of each 2-bar phrase. This breaks up the chord voicing into different sections through simple string grouping. The picking divides the chord into two (or more) registers and allows more variation from a single voicing.

This tune is a burner, so start slow and work it up to tempo, and pretty soon it won't feel like you're such a long way from home!

Long Way From Home

By Stevie Ray Vaughan and Doyle Bramhall

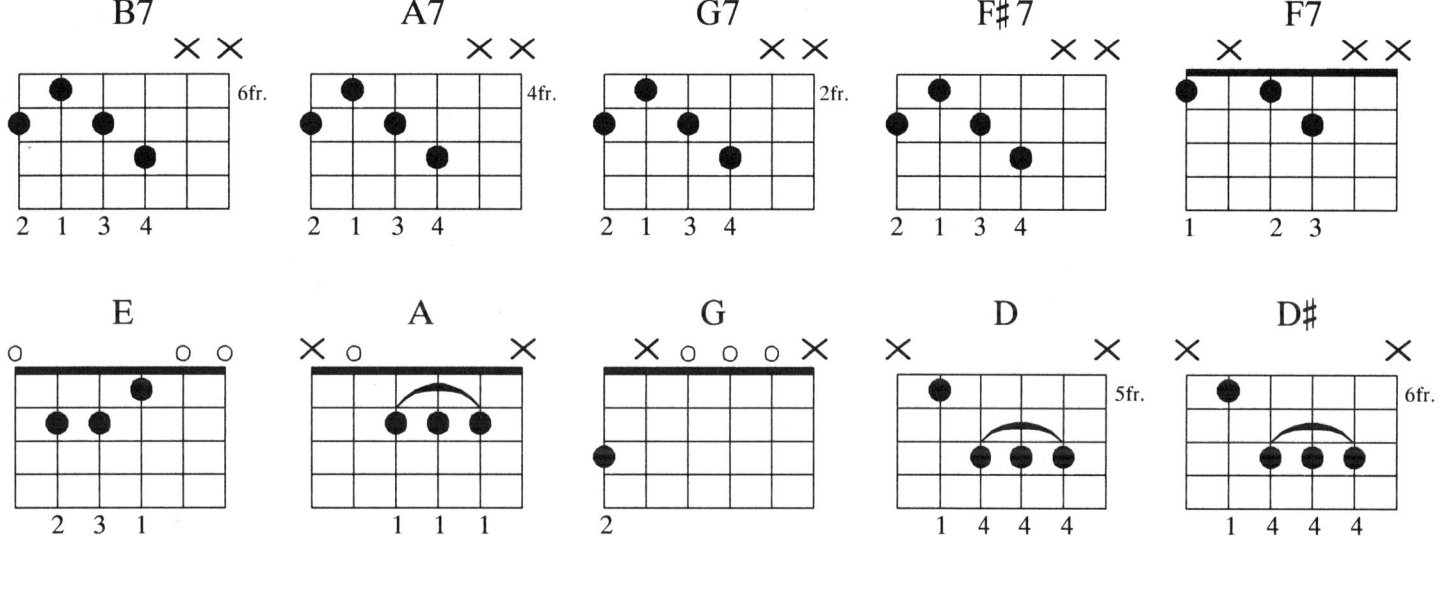

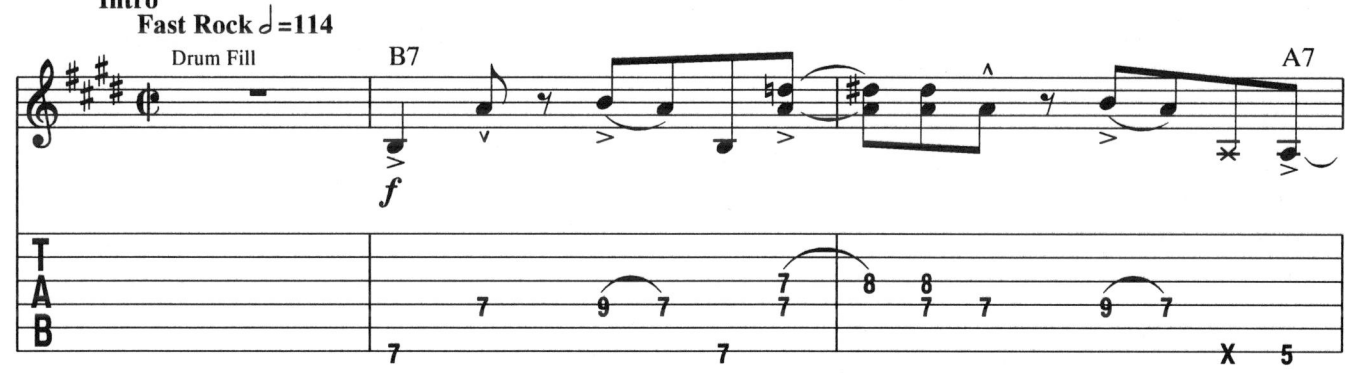

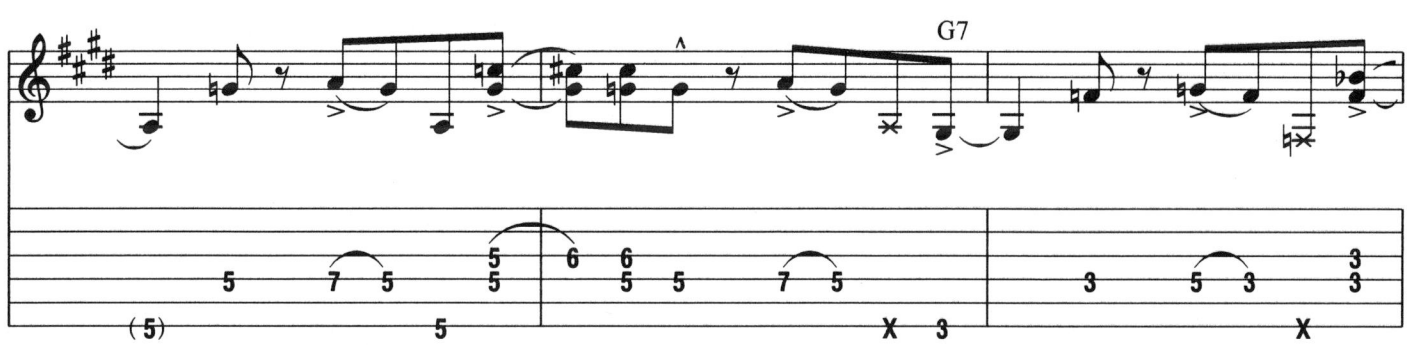

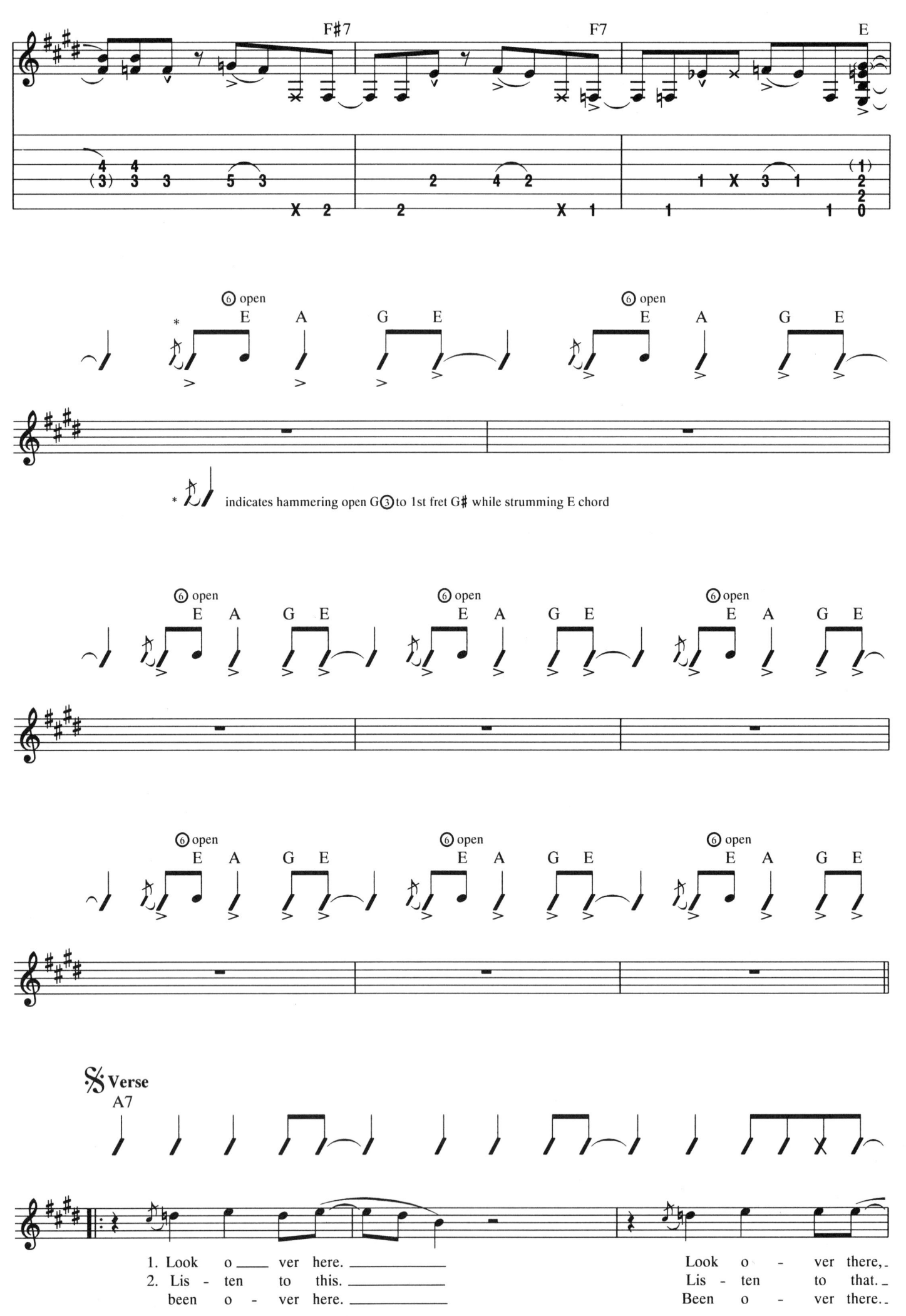

* indicates hammering open G③ to 1st fret G♯ while strumming E chord

1. Look o ____ ver here. _____
2. Lis - ten to this. _____
   been o - ver here. _____

Look o ____ ver there, __
Lis - ten to that. __
Been o - ver there. __

Look   all   a - round ___   me,
Peo-ple try-in'   to   tell ___   me
Friends all   a - round ___   me

E   E   A   G   E

ev - 'ry - where.   Well, it   real - ly   does - n't mat-
where it's   at.   But, it   real - ly   does - n't mat-
ev - 'ry - where.   But, it   real - ly   does - n't mat-

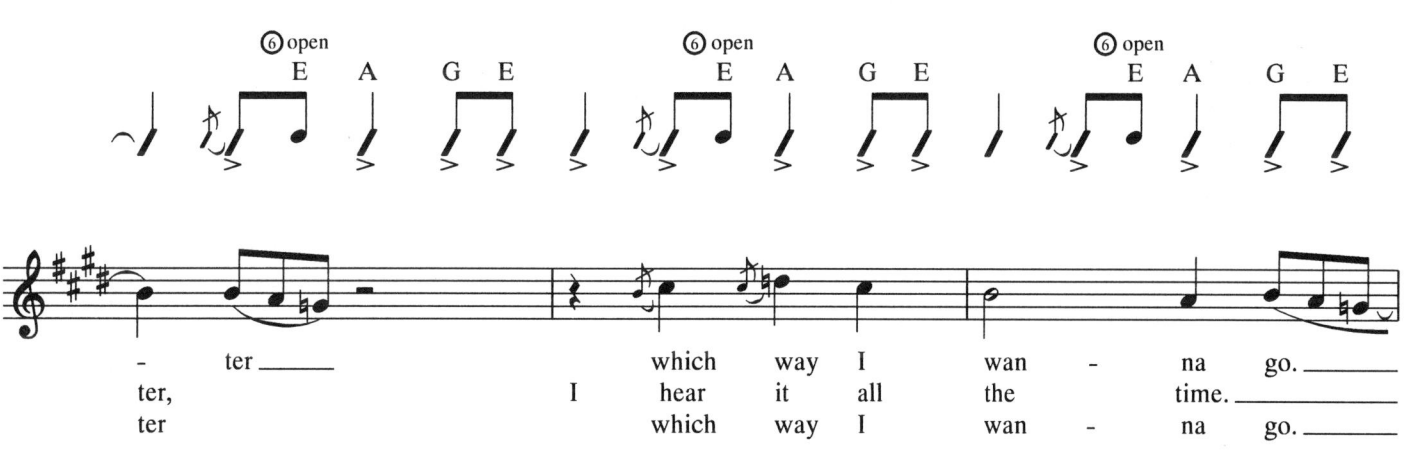

E   A   G   E   E   A   G   E   E   A   G   E

- ter ___   which way I   wan - na go. ___
ter,   I   hear it   all   the   time. ___
ter   which way I   wan - na go. ___

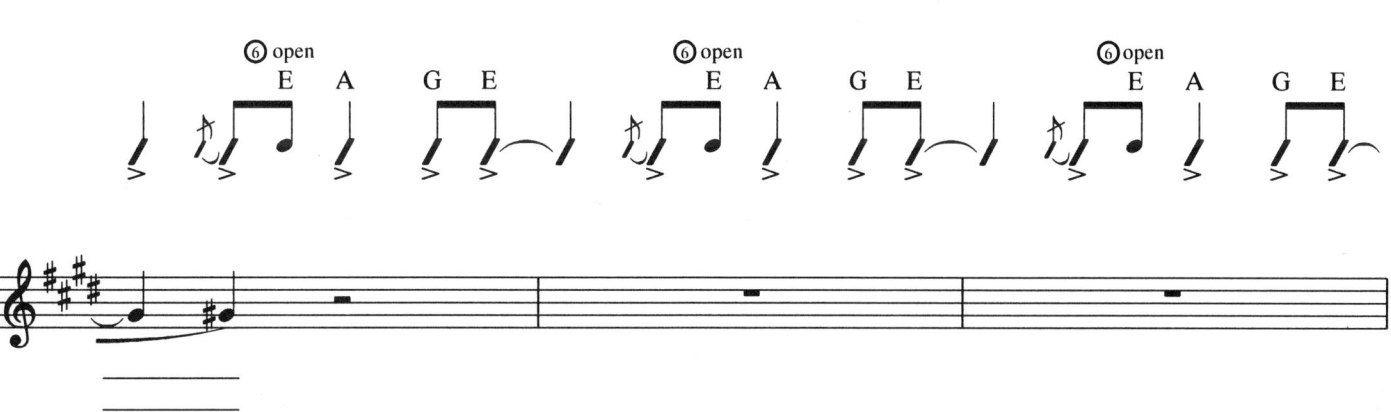

E   A   G   E   E   A   G   E   E   A   G   E

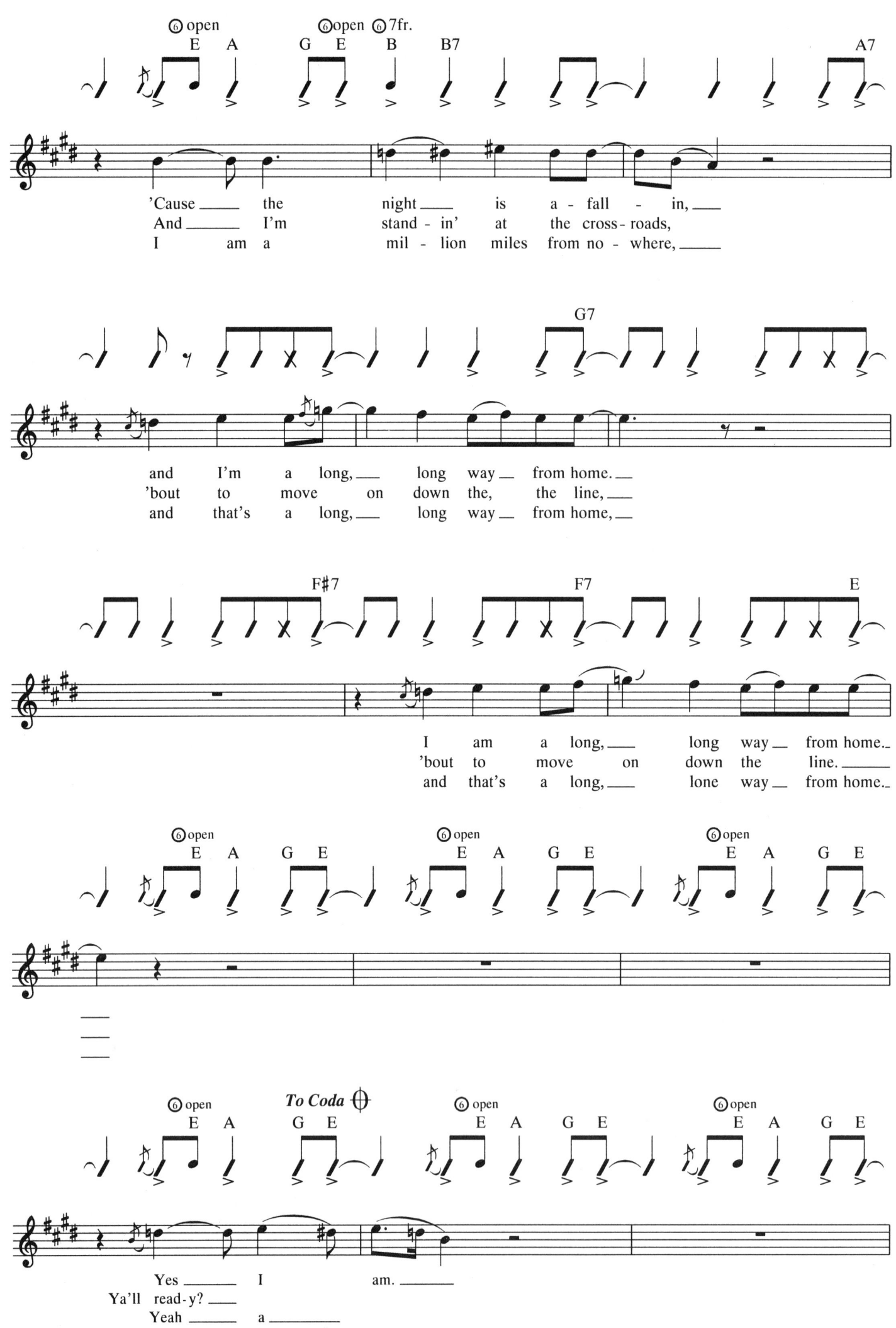

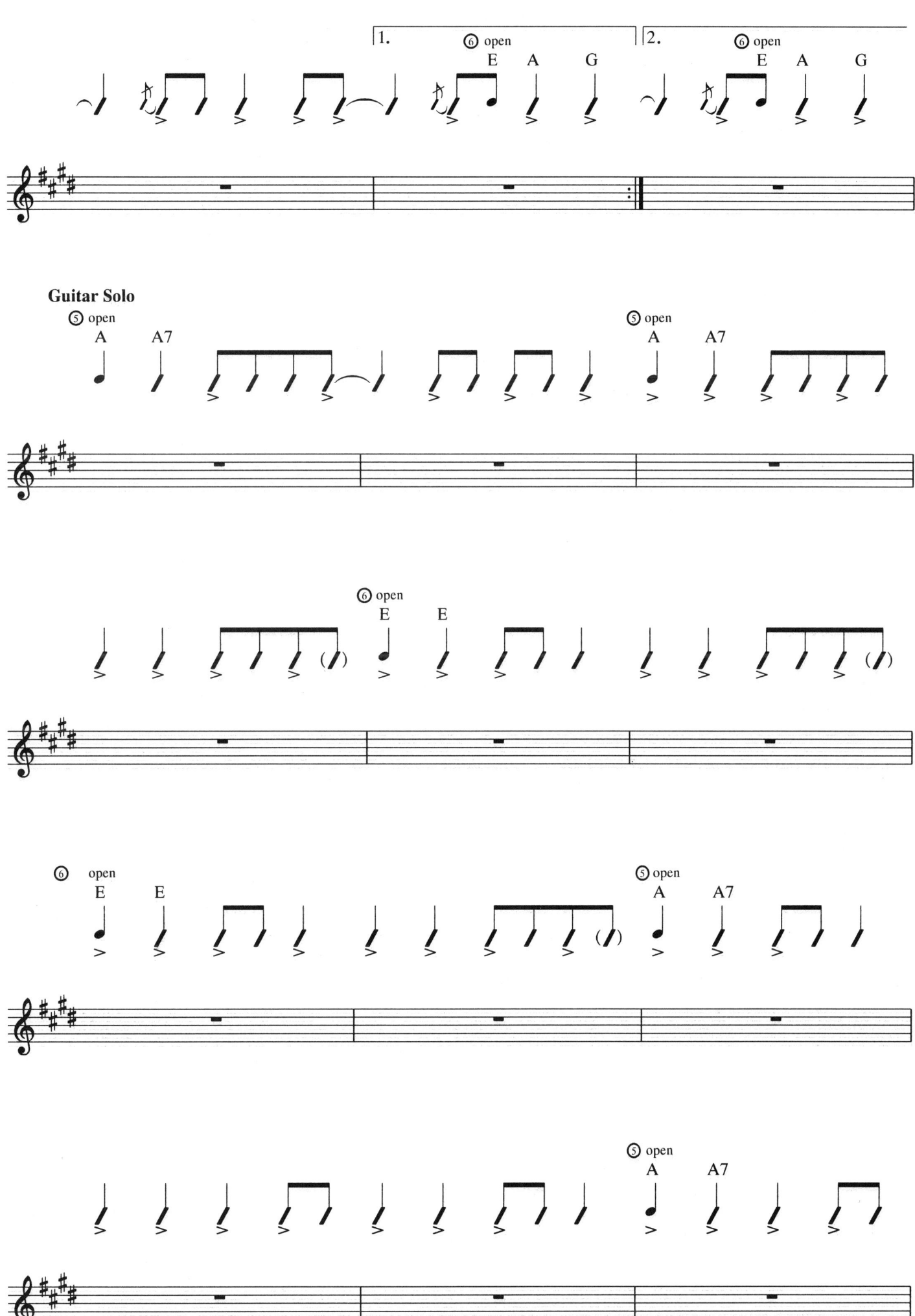

Guitar Solo

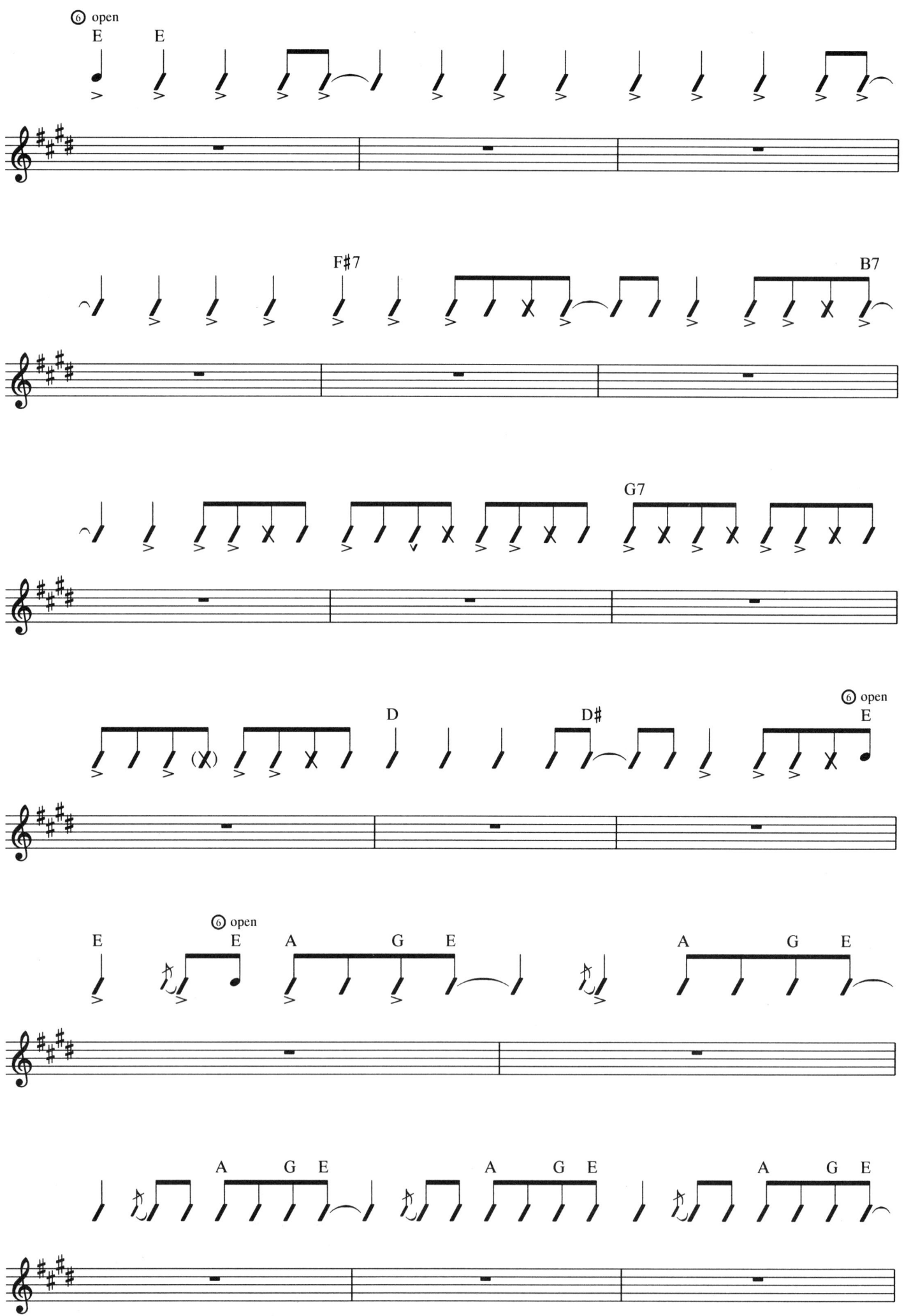

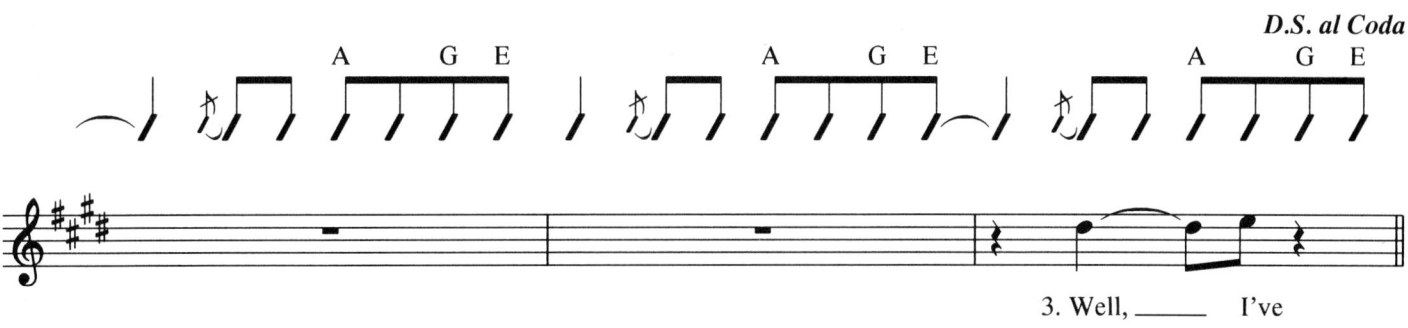

3. Well, ____ I've

Coda

mil - lion miles from no - where, ____ and that's a long,

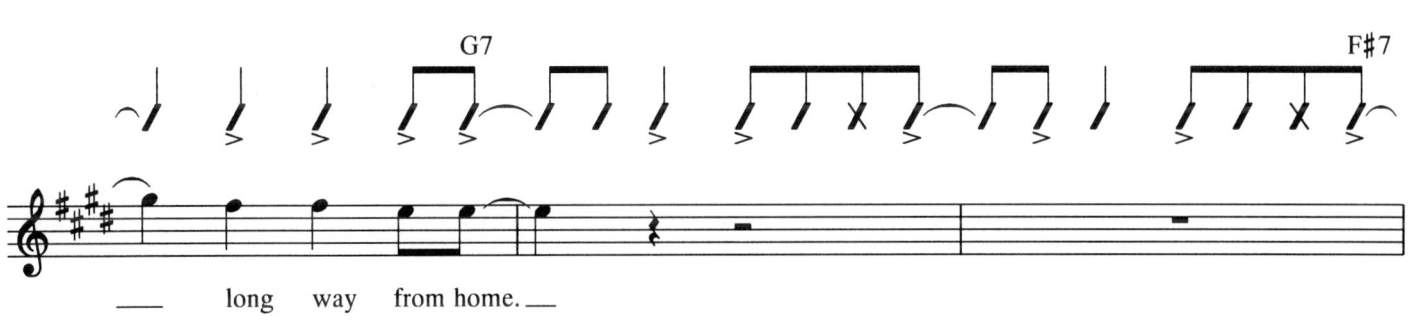

____ long way from home. ____

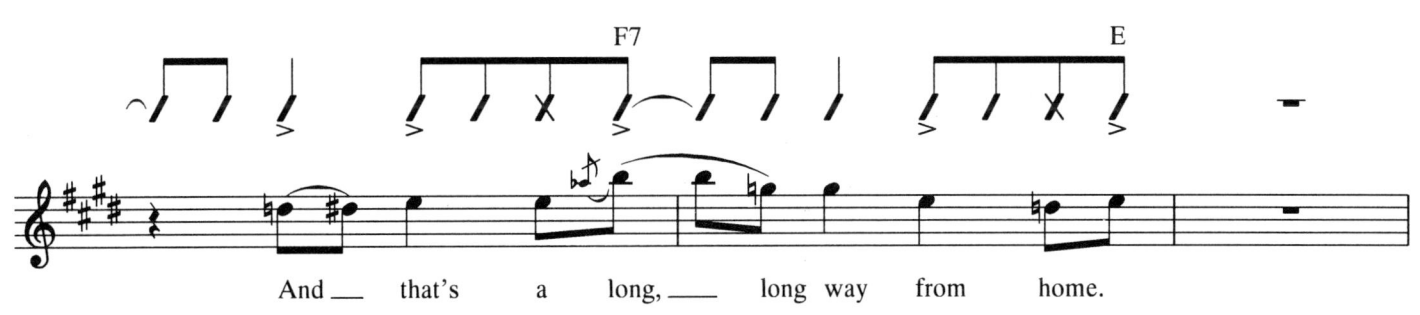

And ____ that's a long, ____ long way from home.

16 Times then Fade

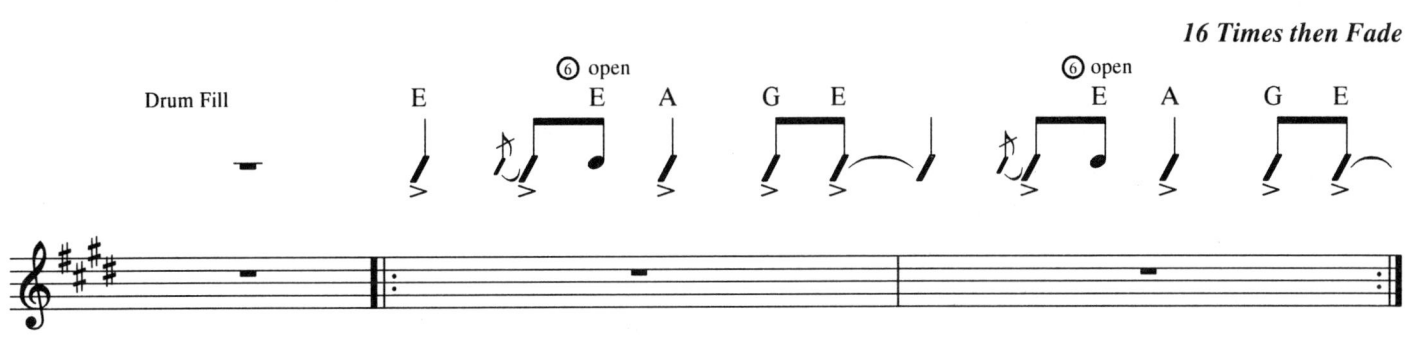

TICK TOCK

LESSON

This beautiful R&B ballad was orchestrated for so many guitars that it was difficult to pick just one that personified the tune. The simple Steve Cropper/Stax-influenced rhythm figure seemed the likeliest candidate, though. After all, its percussive "chicks" not only nail down the backbeat rhythm (accenting beats "2" and "4" with the snare drum), they outline the harmony as well. Again, alternate picking comes into the picture, only this time the pulse is divided into 16th notes keeping this picking pattern consistent:

creates this picking pattern for the repeated 2-bar rhythm figure:

The Pre-chorus figure contains a tricky double stop pull-off lick. Practice picking every note until the figure becomes comfortable, then add the pull-offs. Fingering the 14th fret double stop with a 3rd finger barre sets you up for a comfortable double pull-off to the 1st and 2nd fingers at the 12th and 13th frets respectively. The short Bridge features a new progression and a sliding-6th's interval lick that outlines the G to E chords before sequencing to a short 8-bar solo beginning at bar 68. Here is a good example of thematic development and call and response phrasing. Begin in the 10th position with your 2nd finger on the G string at the 11th fret. This puts the next two notes on the 10th and 12th frets of the B string directly under your 1st and 3rd fingers.

Next, play the grace note slide up to the 14th fret with your 3rd finger and use vibrato to sustain the note. Finally, hammer the same grace note you just played, then re-trace your steps back down the B string to the 10th position. It is easier to shift positions with your 1st finger when descending and your 3rd or 4th finger when ascending.

The fill at bar 76 leads into a reprise of the Pre-chorus and Chorus. Except during the soulful vocal breakdown, the basic rhythm figure repeats through the fadeout.

Tick Tock

By Jimmie Vaughan, Nile Rodgers and Jerry Lynn Williams

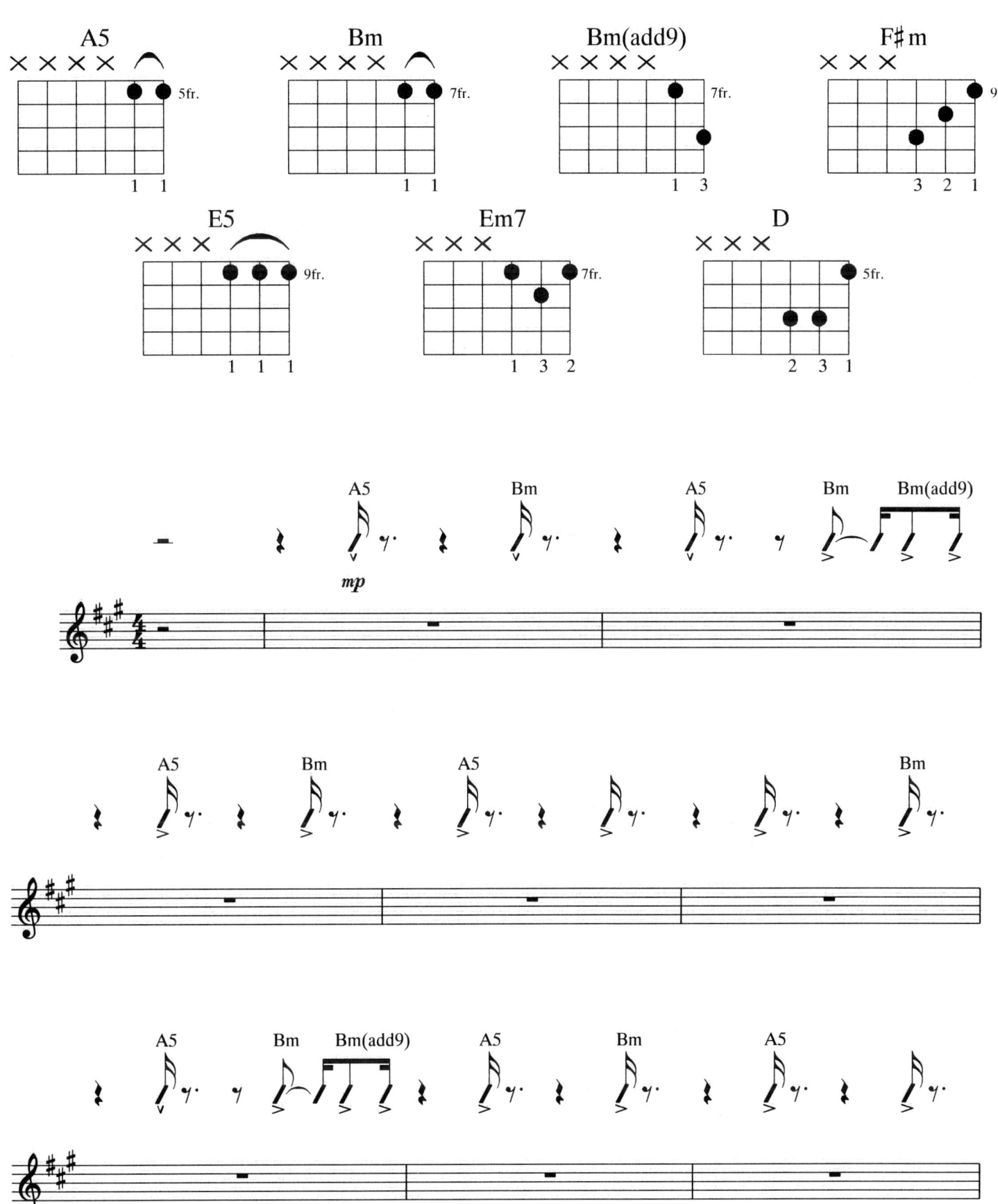

Spoken:
One night while sleeping in my bed, I had a beautiful dream that all the people of the world got together on the same wavelength

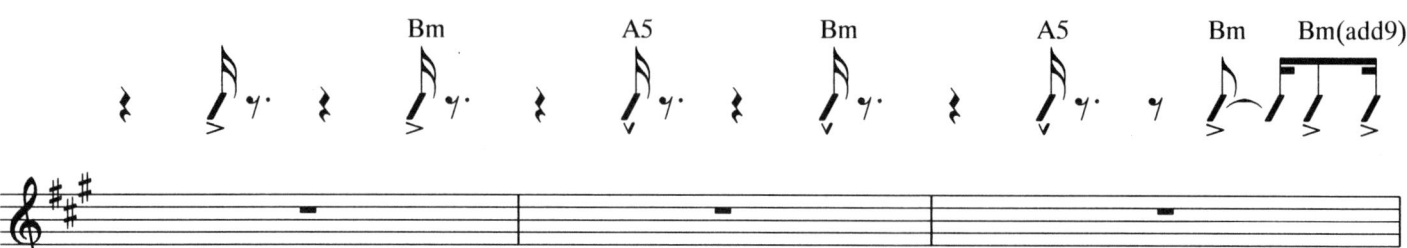

and began helping one another.   Now, in this dream, universal love was the theme of the day.   Peace and

Verse

understanding   and   it   happened   this   way.   1. The sick   and the hun - gry   had

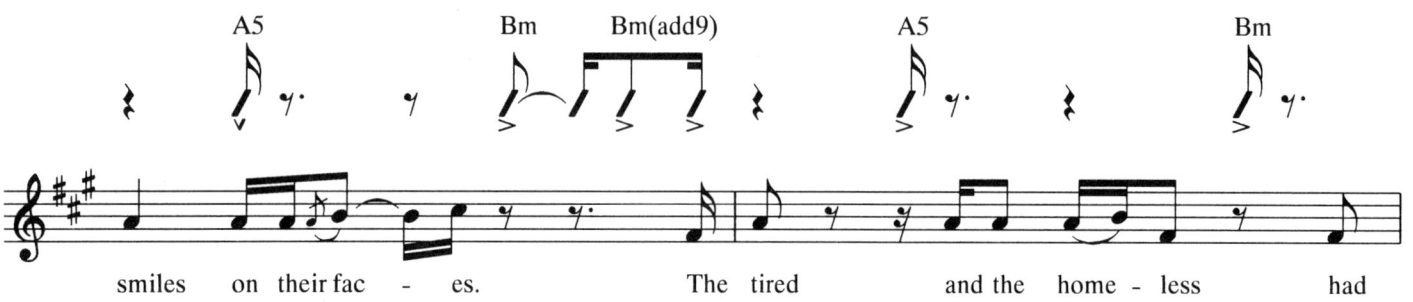

smiles   on their fac - es.   The tired   and the home - less   had

fam - 'ly   all a - round. __   The streets   and the cit - ies   were all

beau-ti-ful plac - es,   and the walls __   came _ tum-bl-in'   down. __   Peo-ple of the world _

Pre-Chorus

all had it to-geth-er, had it to-geth-

-er for the boys and the girls. _____ And the chil-dren of the world

look for-ward to a fu-ture. Re-mem-ber,

Chorus

tick tock, tick tock, tick tock, peo-ple.

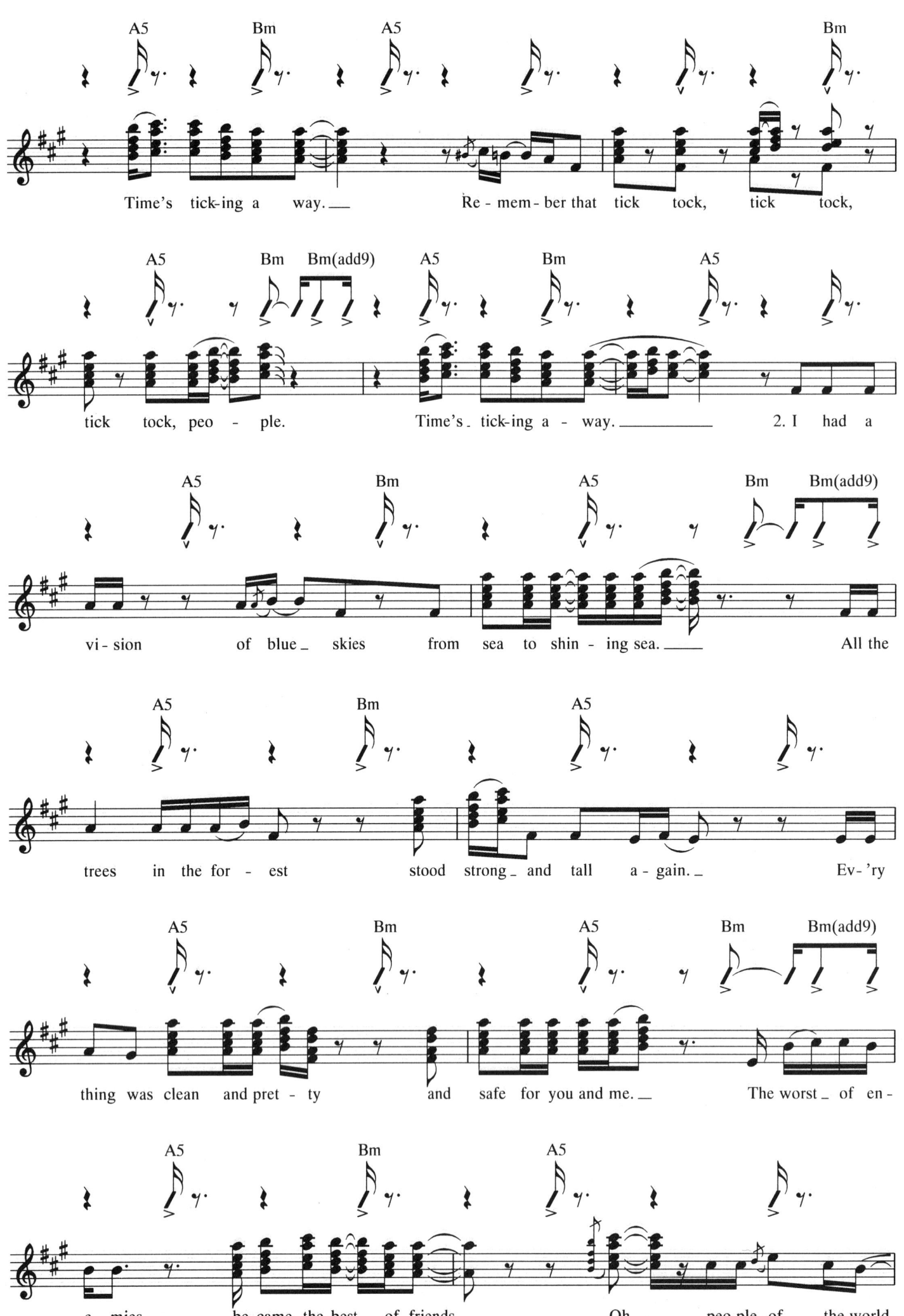

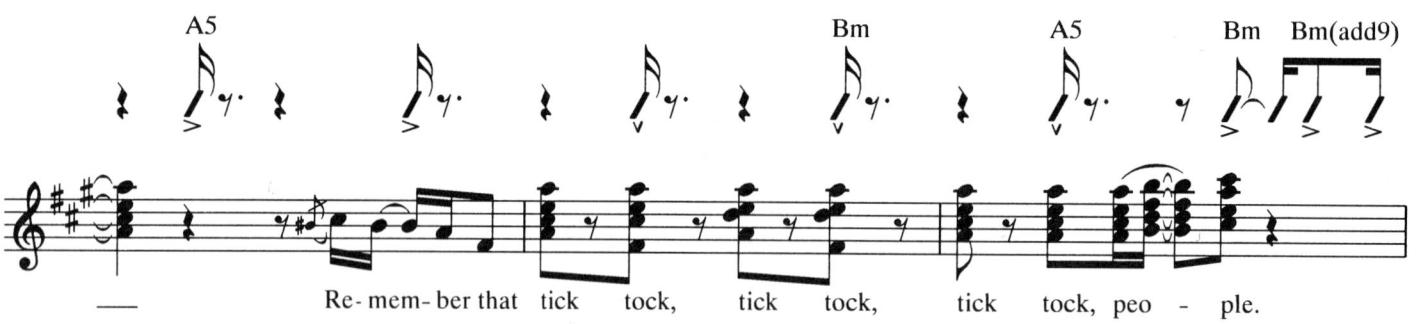

Re-mem-ber that tick tock, tick tock, tick tock, peo - ple.

To Coda ⊕

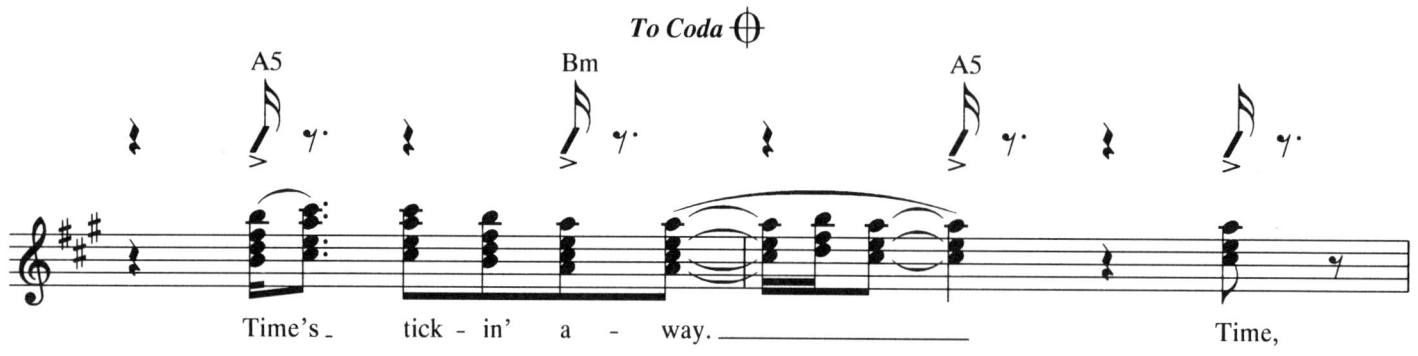

Time's _ tick - in' a - way. _____ Time,

Bridge

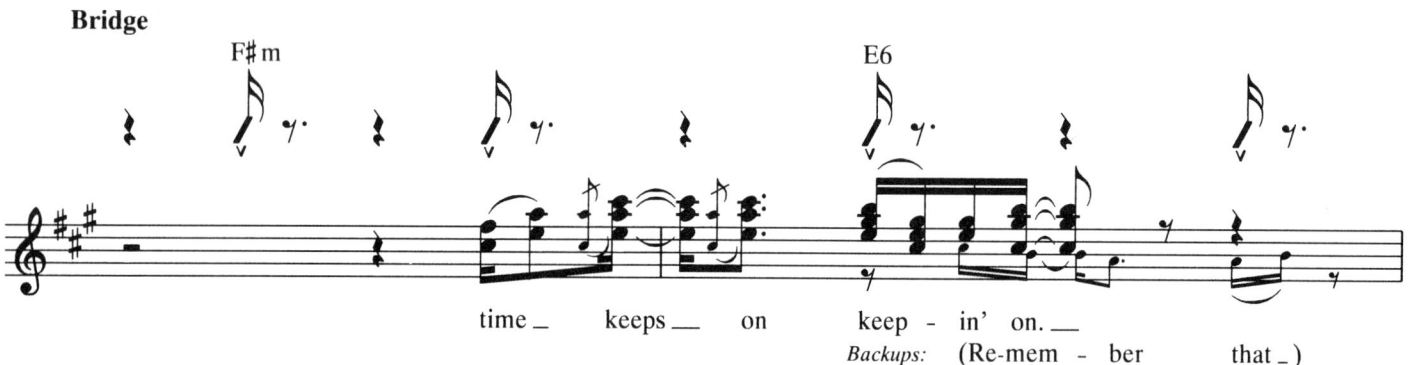

time _ keeps _ on keep - in' on. _
Backups: (Re - mem - ber that _)

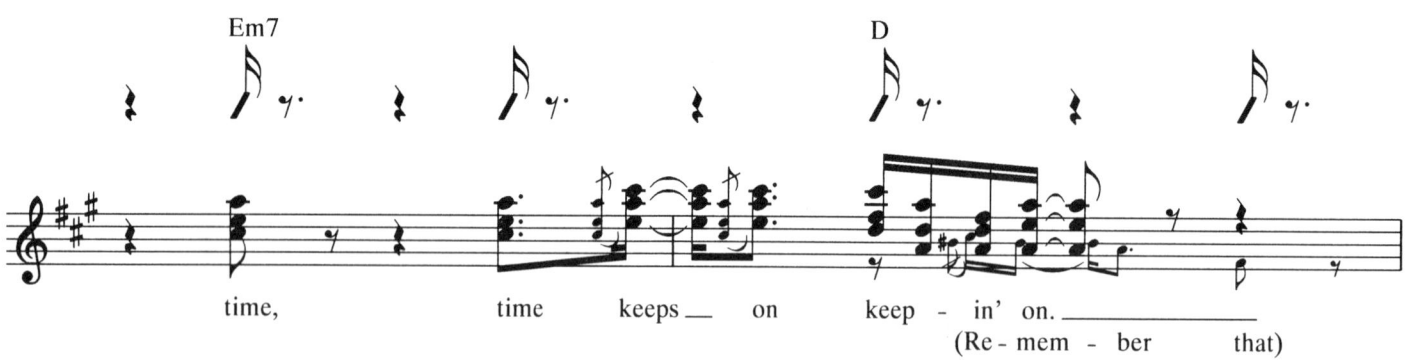

time, time keeps _ on keep - in' on. _
(Re - mem - ber that)

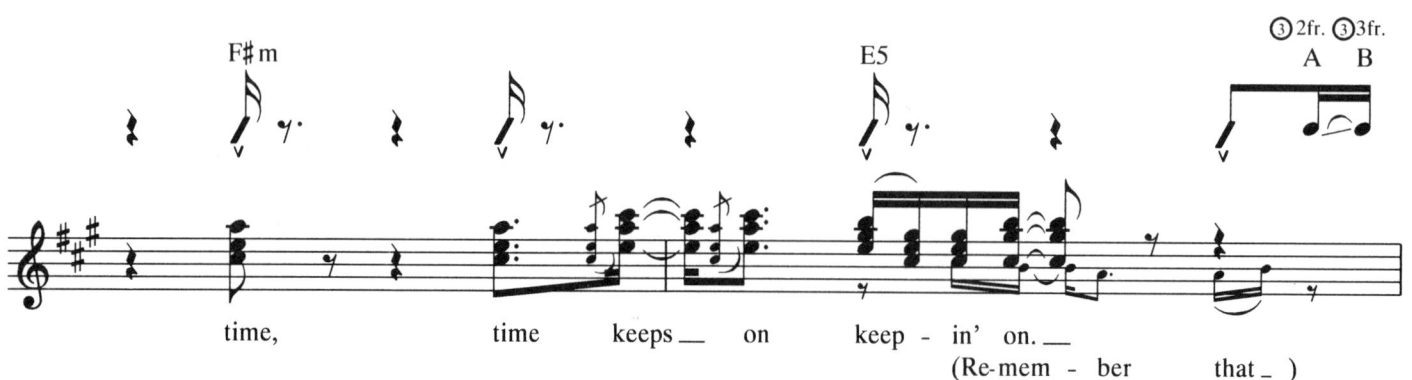

time, time keeps _ on keep - in' on. _
(Re - mem - ber that _)

66

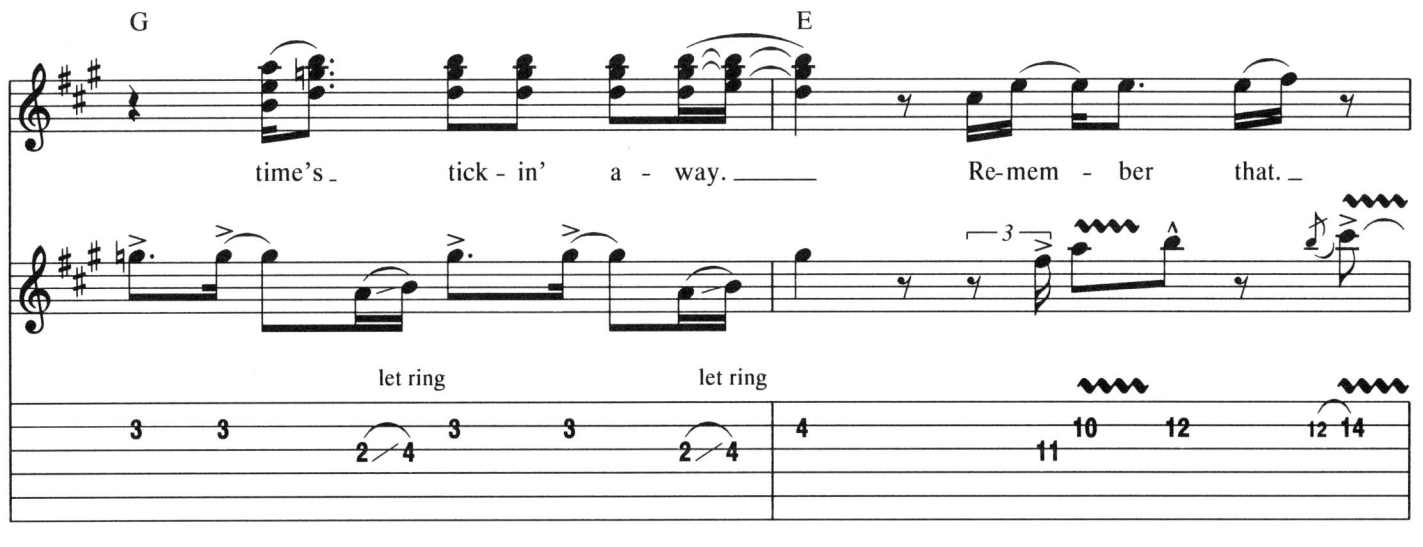

time's tick-in' a - way._____ Re-mem-ber that.__

Guitar Solo

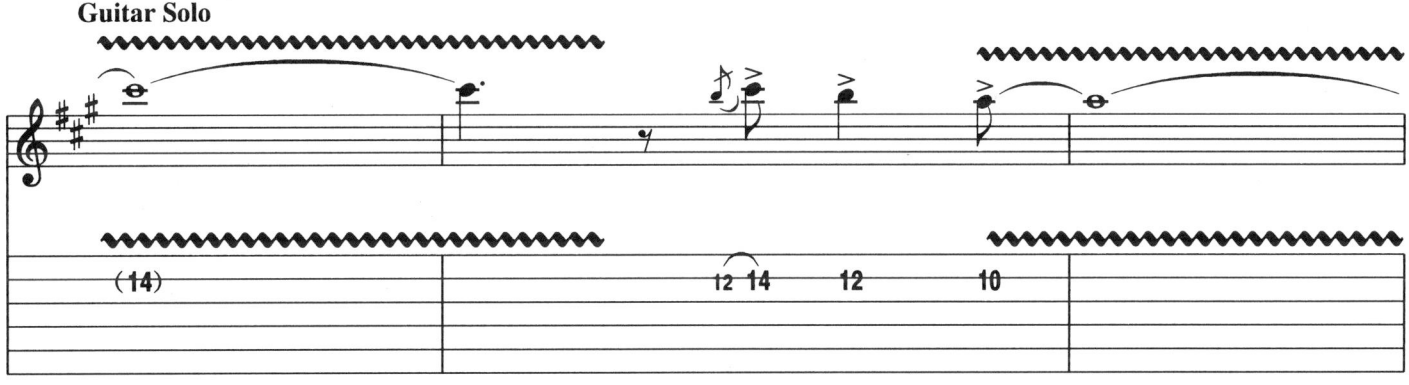

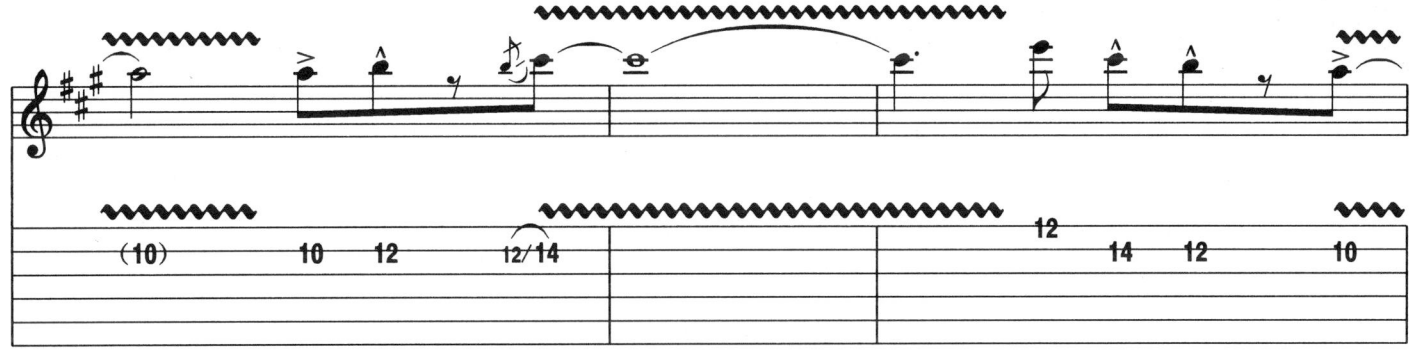

D.S. al Coda

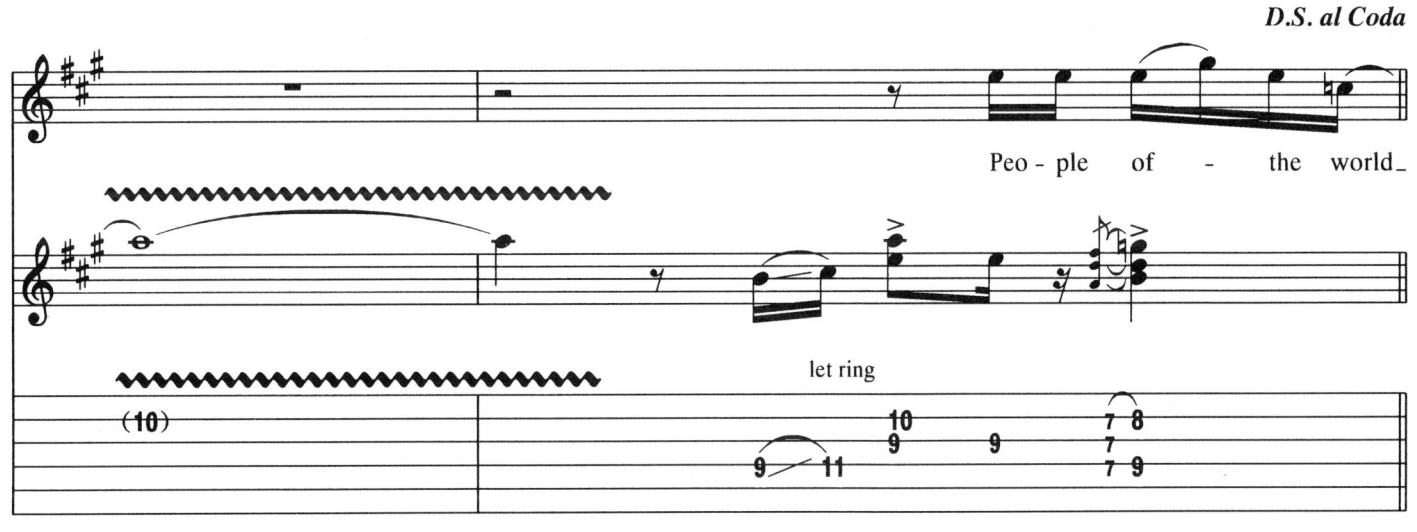

Peo - ple of - the world__

⊕ *Coda*

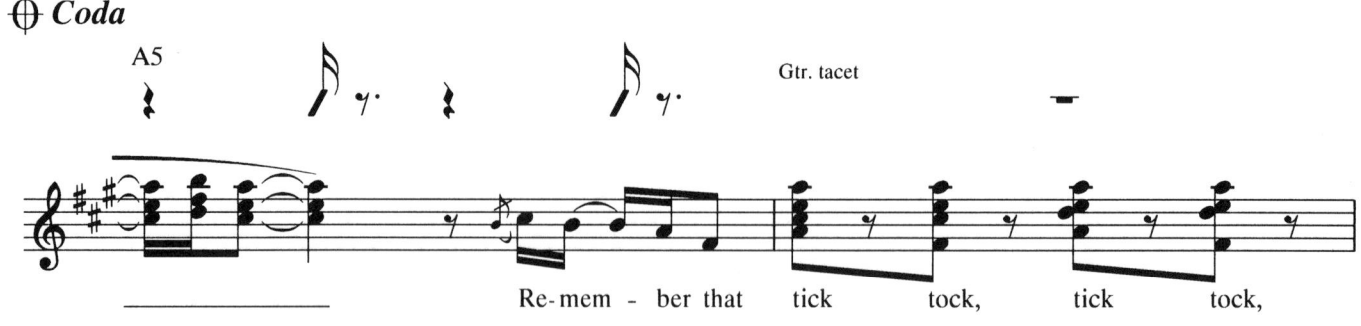

Re-mem - ber that tick tock, tick tock,

tick tock, peo - ple. Time's _ tick-in' a - way. ___ Re-mem - ber

tick tock, tick tock, tick tock, peo - ple.

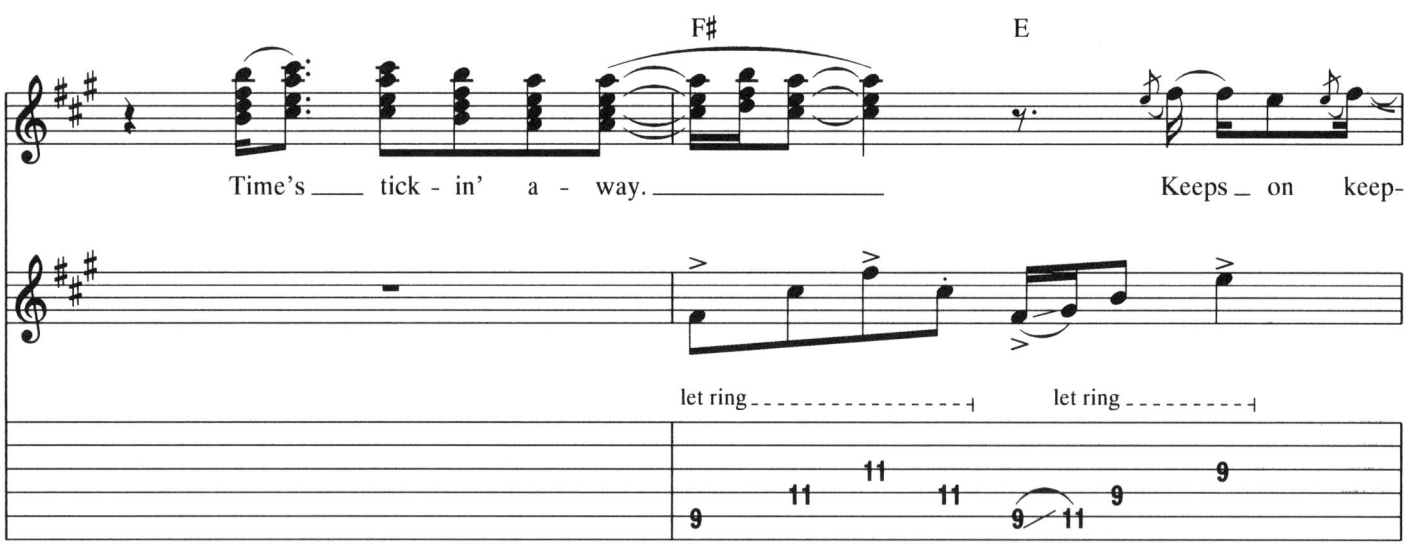

Time's ___ tick-in' a - way. _____ Keeps _ on keep-

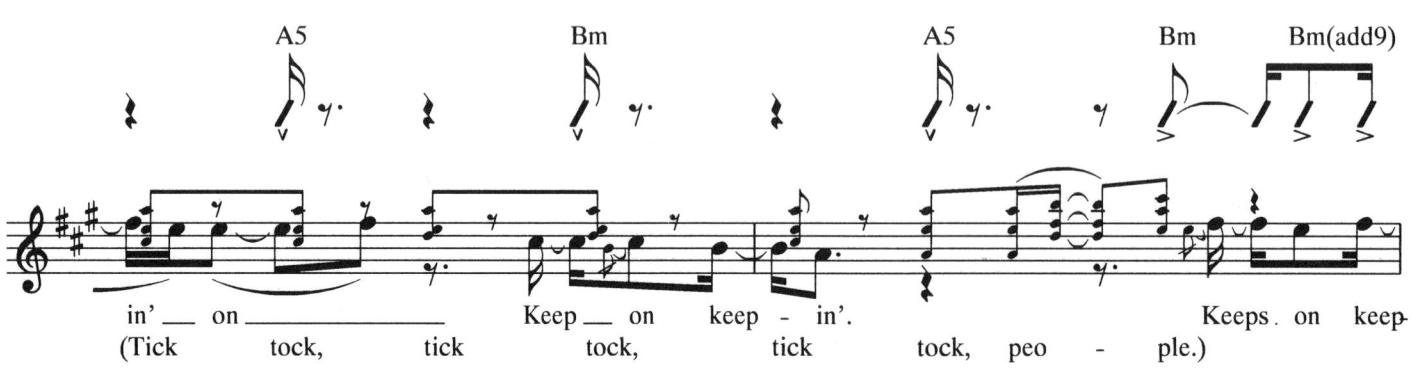

in' ___ on _____ Keep _ on keep - in'. Keeps _ on keep-

(Tick tock, tick tock, tick tock, peo - ple.)

TELEPHONE SONG

LESSON

"Telephone Song" casts its funky Hendrix spell from bar one. The secret to the power behind this rhythm figure is, you guessed it...alternate picking!

As it is in "Tick Tock," the beat is divided into 16th notes and your picking hand should loosen up and feel the groove in the same manner. The Intro figure is most comfortably picked as follows:

Stevie Ray Vaughan often experimented with many "against-the-grain" picking patterns though, so once you've got alternate picking down, don't hesitate to break the mold!

Applying the same concept to bar 2 yields these results:

Again, only add ornamentations such as hammer-ons, grace-notes and vibrato after you are comfortable picking every note at a slow, even tempo. Remember that hammer-ons and pull-offs replace pickstrokes and adapt alternate picking patterns accordingly. If this gives you an exceptionally hard time, try filling in all non-picked 16th beats with muted "chicks" and have yourself a funk fiesta while getting the part skin tight!

The unison bass line in bar 9 leads into the Verse rhythm figure filled with syncopations (accented upbeats). Alternate picking will once again keep you from losing the groove. The 1-bar rhythm motif is repeated throughout the Verse, and the 9th chords are moveable forms, so it shouldn't take too long to get a handle on this one. Those low octave E's (actually E♭'s due to Stevie Ray Vaughan's dropped 1/2 step tuning) really drive the part and are re-approached via a grace hammer from flat 3 to 3, a bluesy flat 7 and two quick 9th chord punctuations borrowed from brother Jimmie's part.

The chords as well as the octave bass notes are omitted when the riff is re-shaped for the 7th position B and 5th position A chords. The following F# lick (II chord) in the 2nd position thins out considerably and moves back to the 7th position B riff before returning to the tonic E figure.

The Solo rhythm figure is chock-full-o'-syncopations á la Jimmy Nolen/James Brown. Dig the slurred 1/2 step repeats, so once you achieve rhythmic stability most of the work is in the fretting hand.

Note again how the bass note and chord are broken up in the urgent conclusion to the Solo (bars 66 and 67). The B^7#9 also adds more sting than the tamer B^9.

Telephone Song

By Stevie Ray Vaughan and Doyle Bramhall

Tune Down 1/2 Step

(4)=D♭ (1)=E♭

(5)=A♭ (2)=B♭

(6)=E♭ (3)=G♭

Intro

Moderate Rock ♩=118

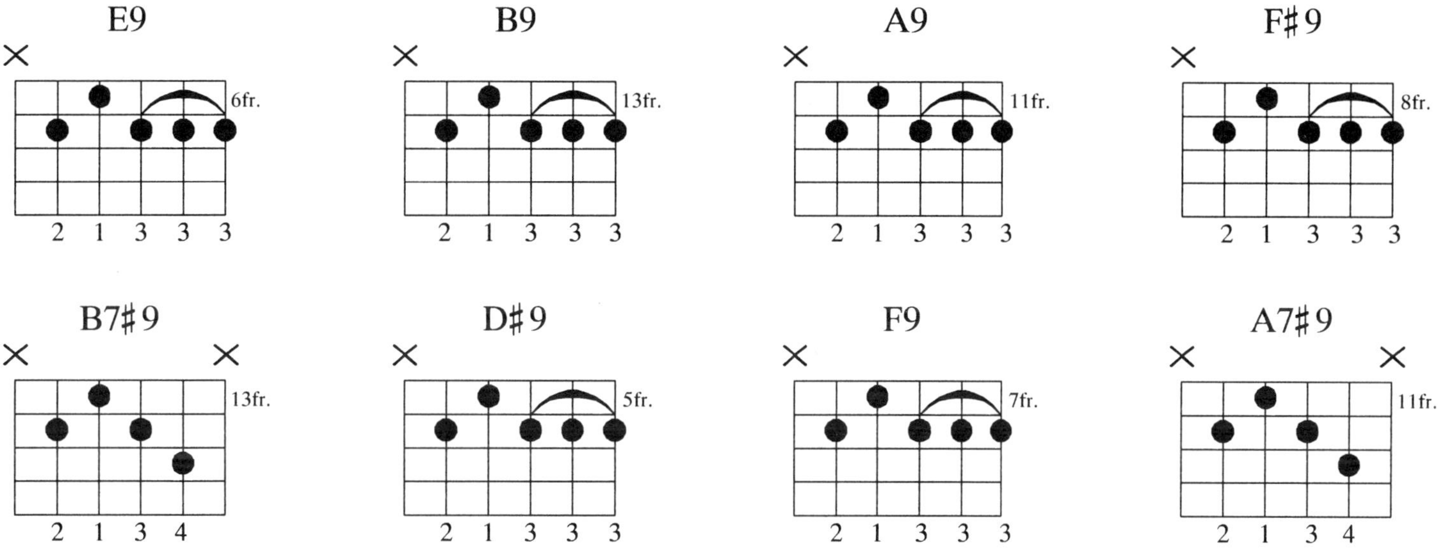

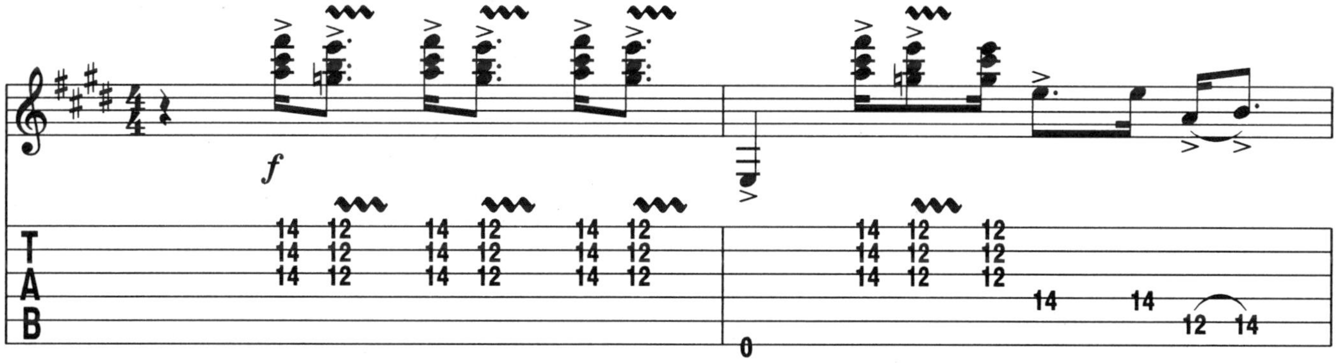

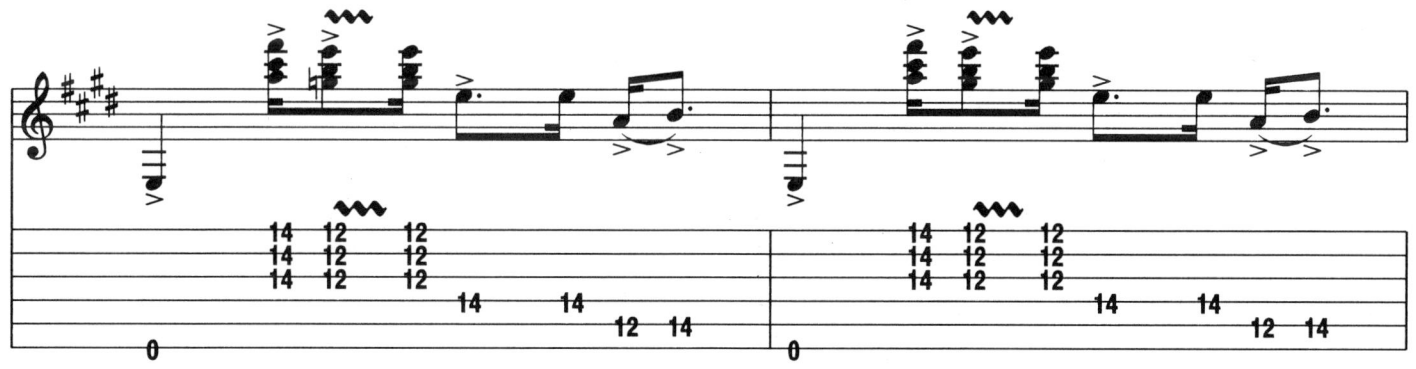

Verse

E9

1. Woke up this morn - in', I was all a - lone.

Saw ____ your pic - ture by the tel - e - phone.

B9

I ____ was miss-in' you ____ oh ____ so bad. ____

Wish ____ I had you here to hold. ____

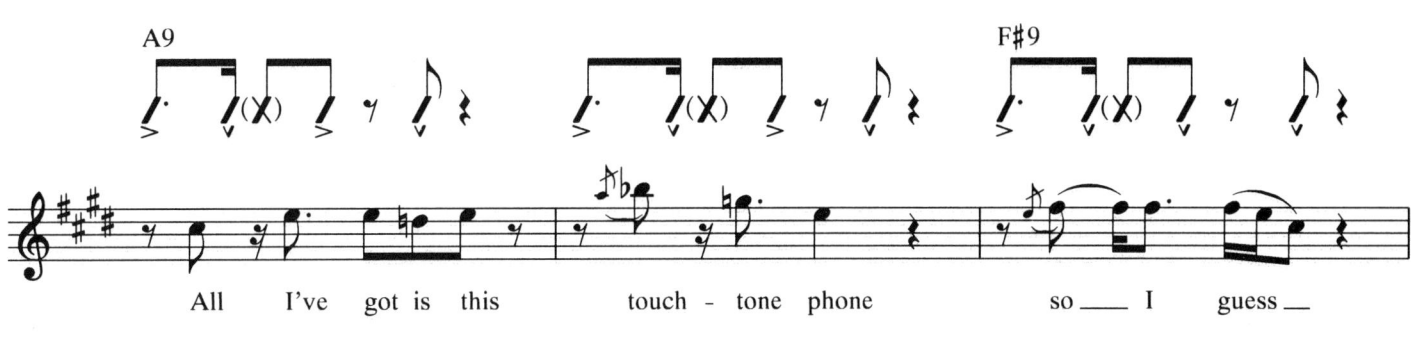

All I've got is this touch - tone phone so ___ I guess ___

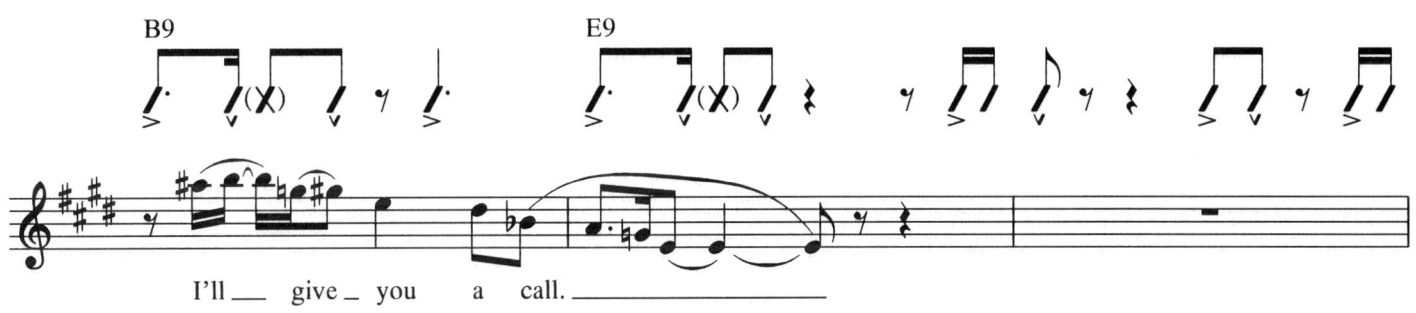

I'll ___ give ___ you a call. _____

w/ Rhy. Fig. 1

Verse

2. Op - er - a - tor, help ___ me please ___
3. Woke up this morn-ing, I was all a - lone. ___

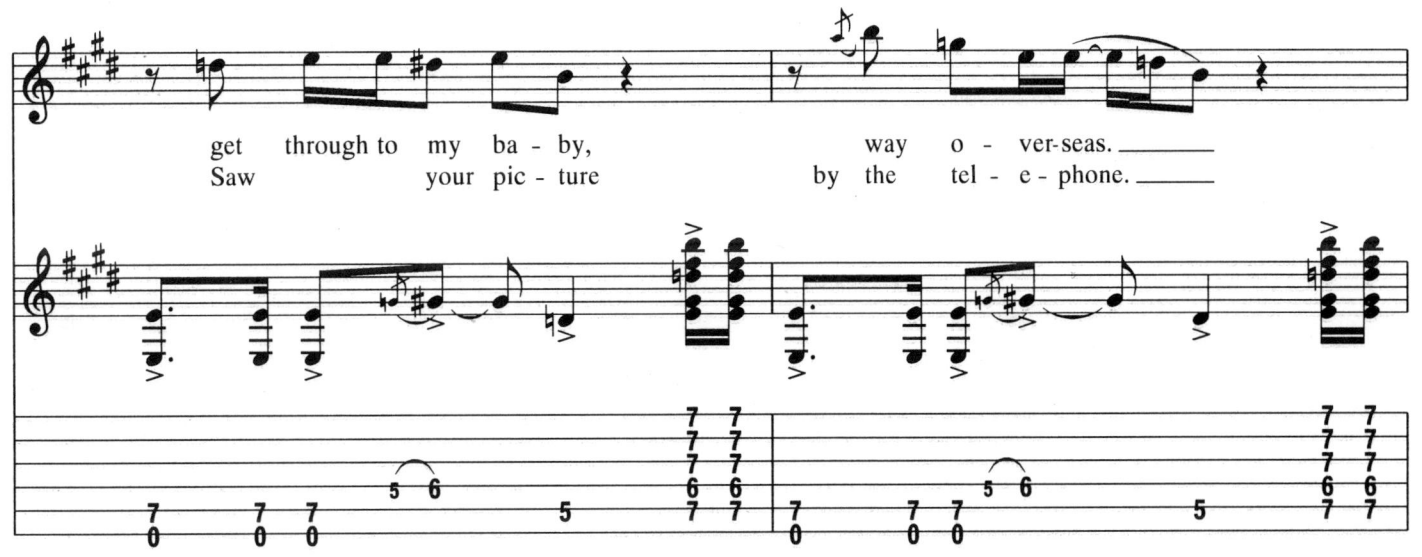

get through to my ba - by, way o - ver-seas. _____
Saw your pic - ture by the tel - e - phone. _____

Time's ___ a - wast - in',   oh, _____ so fast. ___
I've been miss ing you, ba - by,   oh, _____ so bad. ___

Hel - lo ba - by, tell me is that you? _____
I love you ba - by, with all my might. _

I _____ don't know what we're gon - na do,
Come _____ on home and squeeze _____ me tight.

but _____ for now _____ I'm _____ glad _____ I got you on _____ the line..
Long dis - tance lov - in' gon - na drive me out of my

To Coda ⊕

mind. _____

Well, _____ it

Bridge

feels _ so fine _____ know-in' you're _ al - right, _____

_____ but _ you're miles _ a - way. ___ Lord, _ it's not _ the

same. _____

Guitar Solo

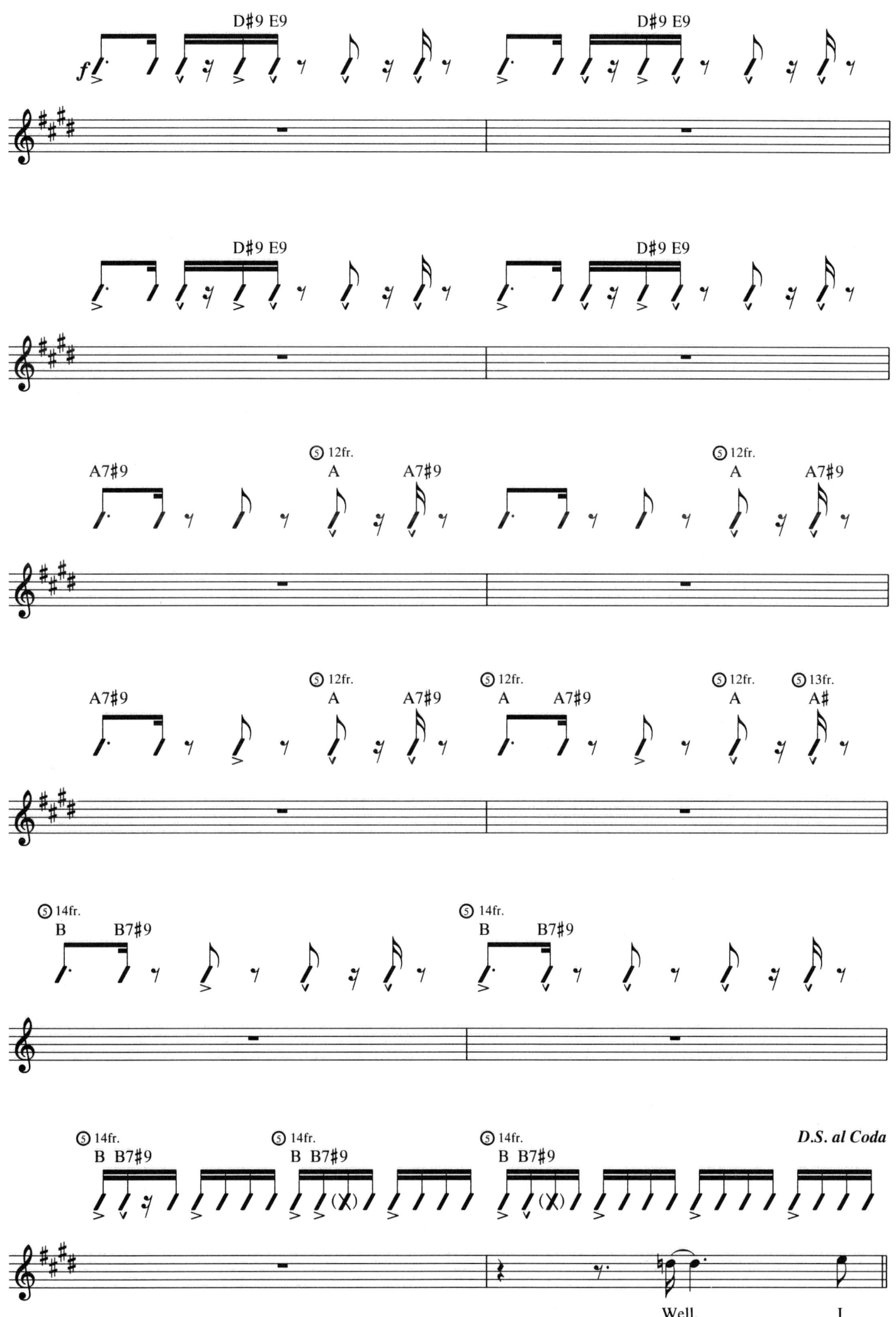

D.S. al Coda

Well,   I

⊕ **Coda**

Spoken: You bet-ter come on __ home ba - by.   I'm 'bout to go cra-zy!

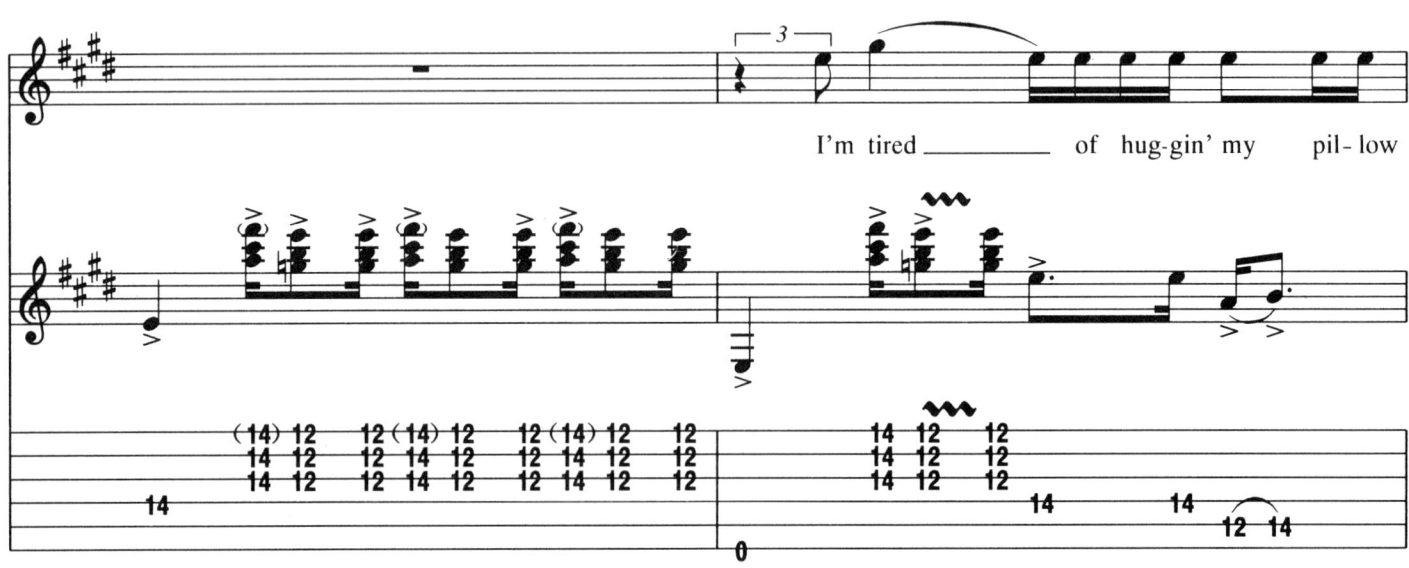

I'm tired _____ of hug-gin' my   pil-low

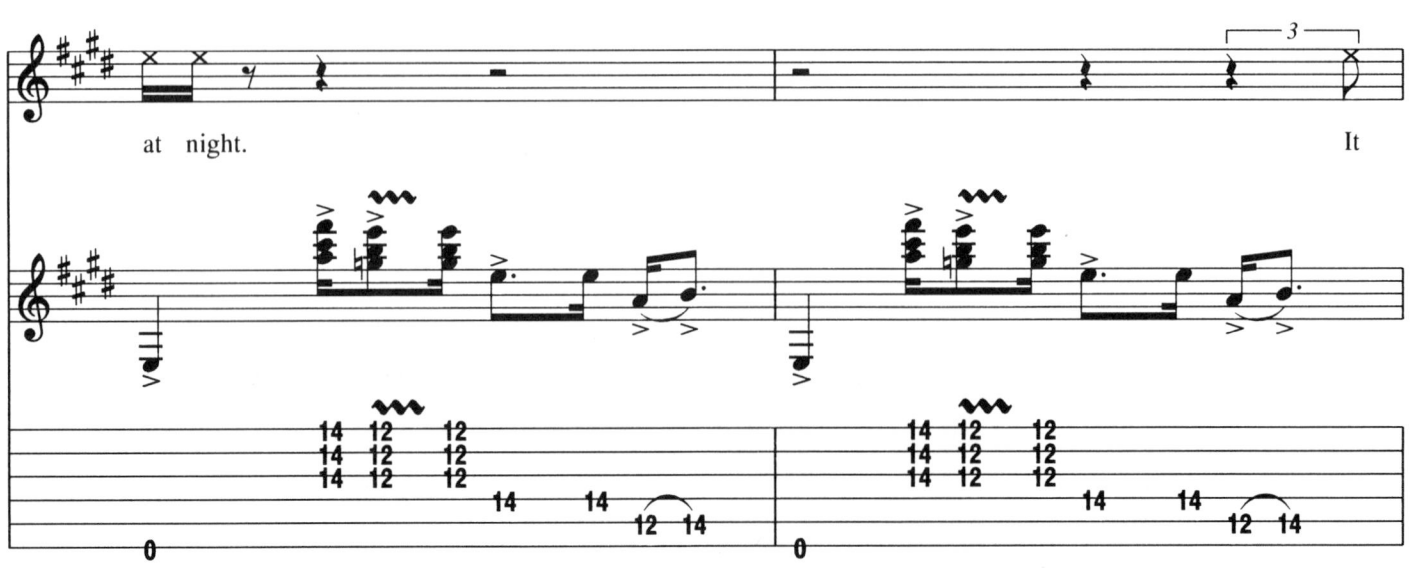

at night.   It

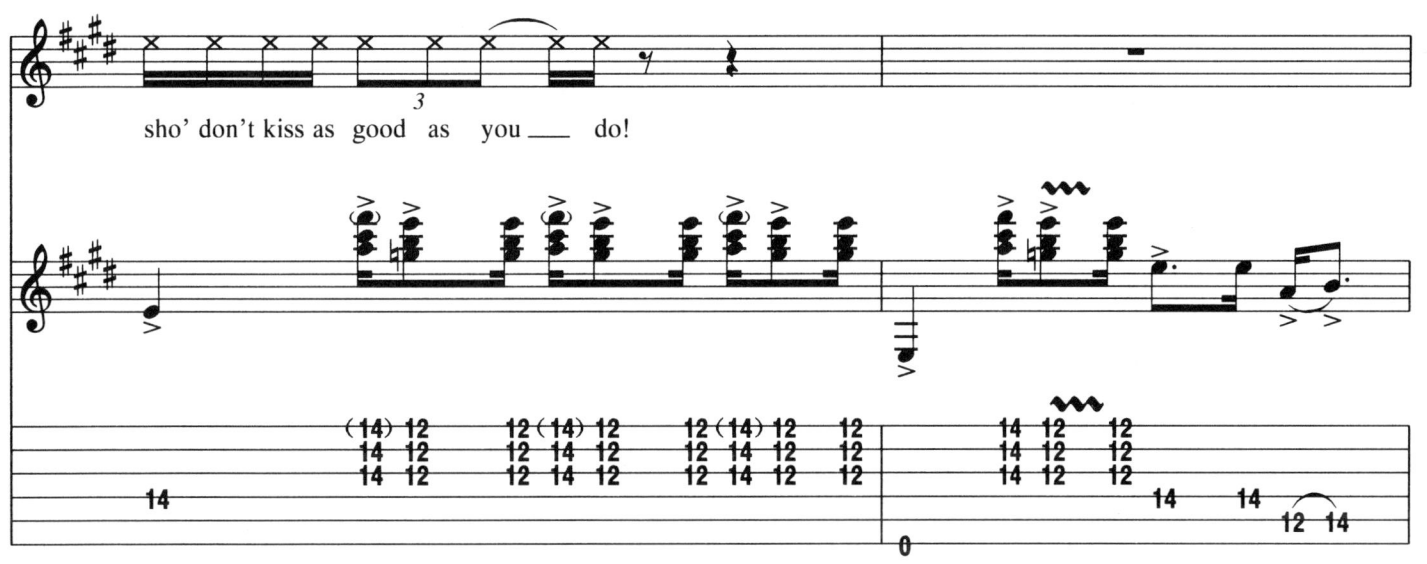

sho' don't kiss as good as you __ do!

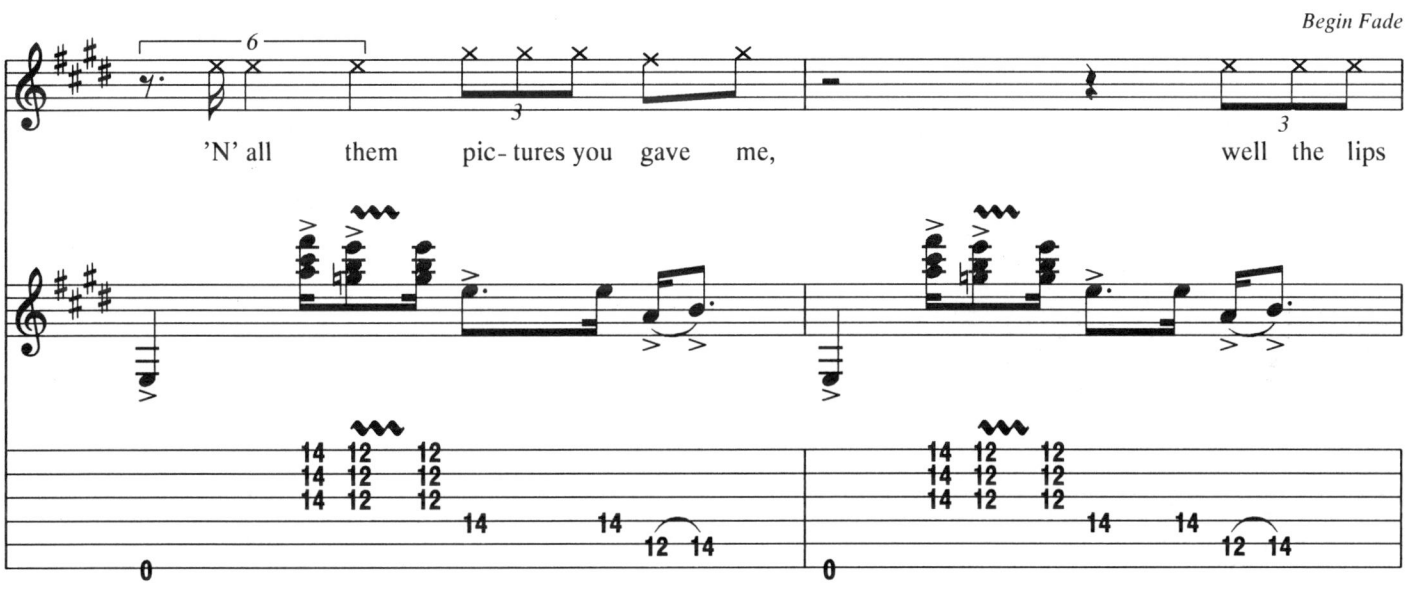

Begin Fade

'N' all them pic- tures you gave me,   well the lips

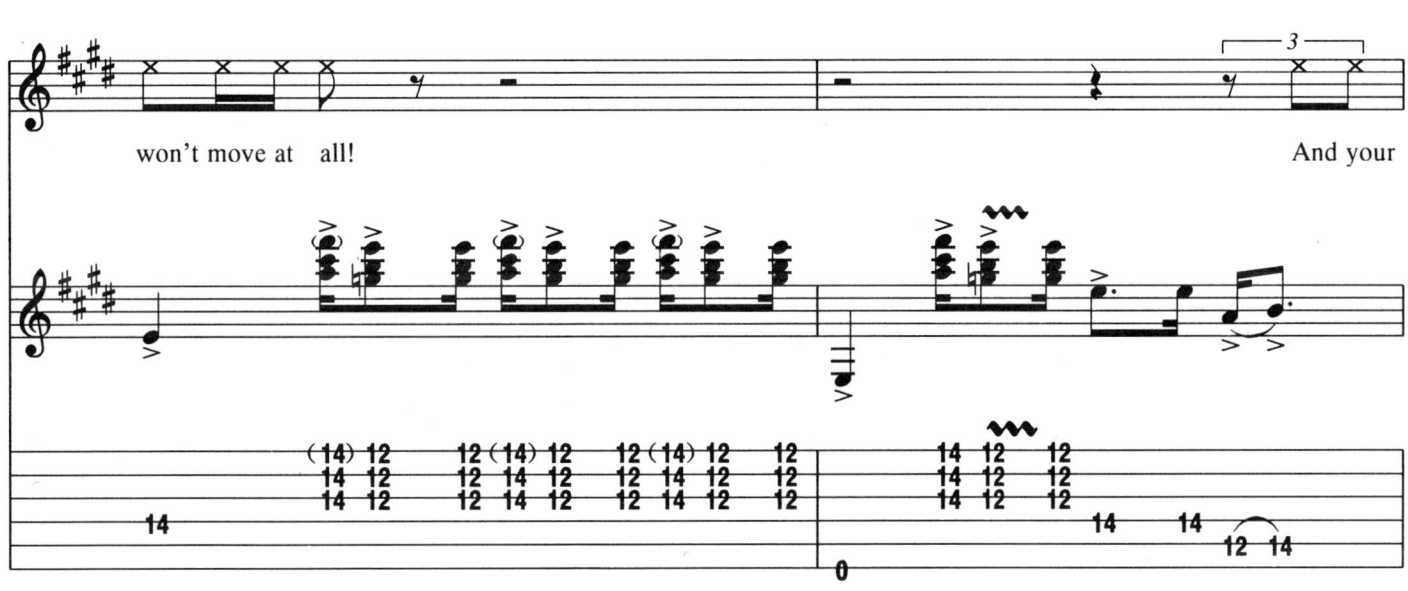

won't move at all!   And your

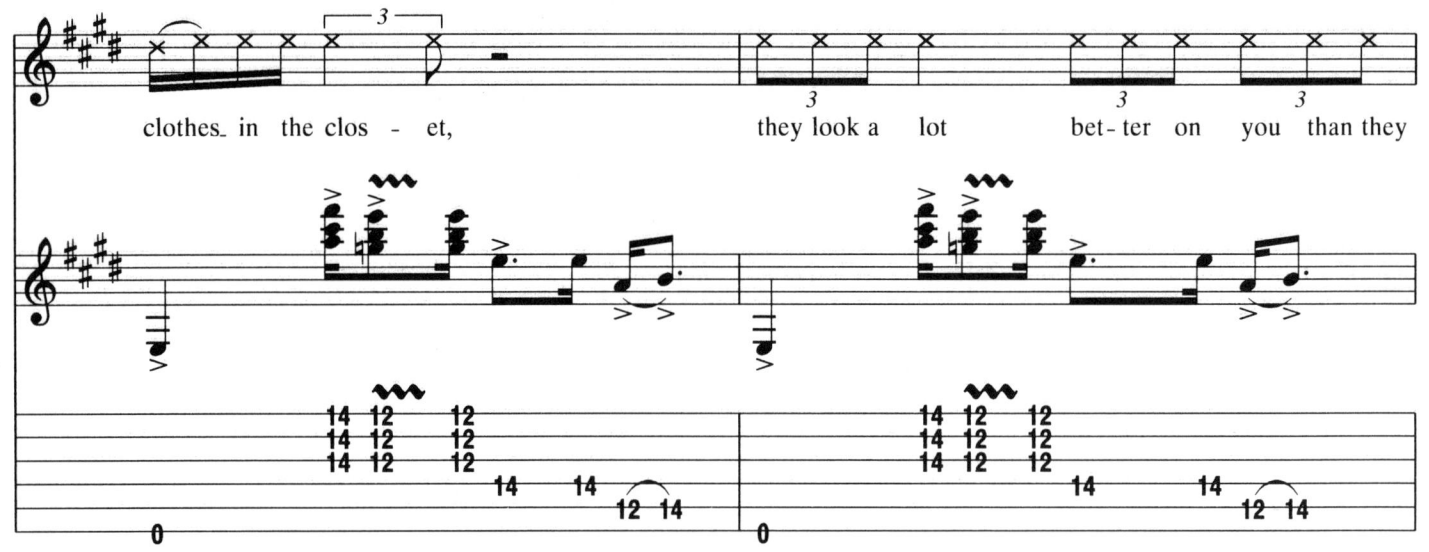

clothes_ in the clos - et,   they look a   lot   bet - ter on   you than they

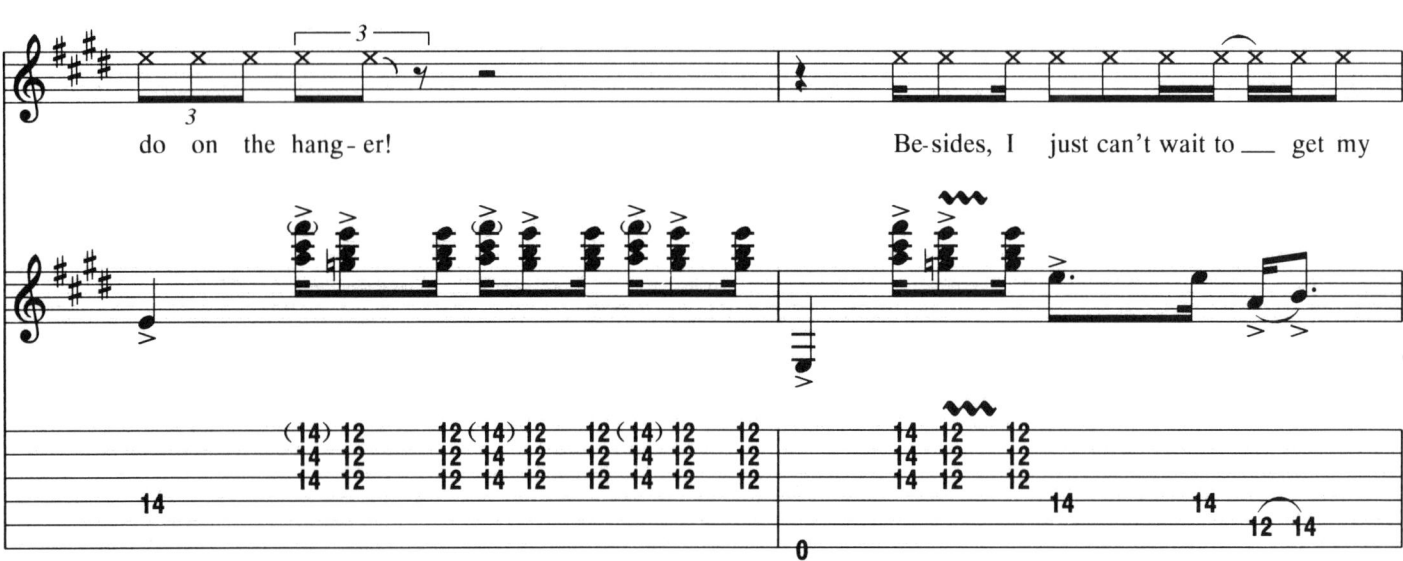

do   on the hang - er!   Be-sides, I   just can't wait to __ get my

Fade

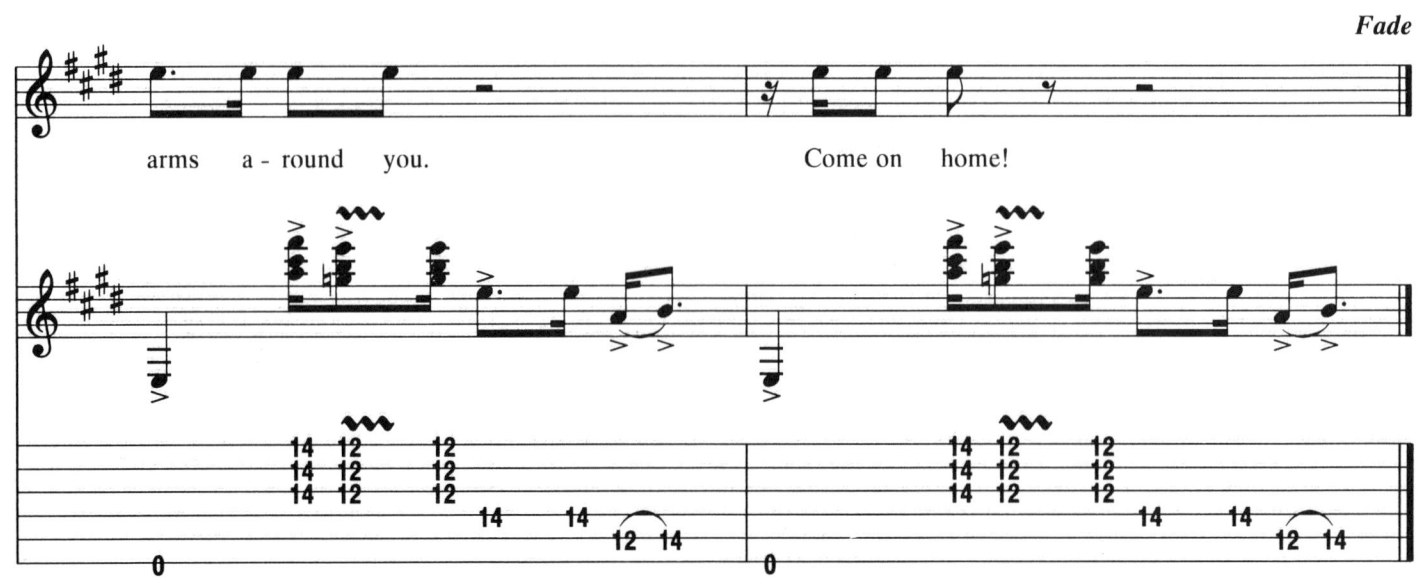

arms a - round you.   Come on   home!

BABOOM/ MAMA SAID

LESSON

The most parts-oriented tune of the lot, "Baboom/Mama Said" provides a virtual textbook of the Jimmy Nolen school of James Brown funk.

The main figure here was actually played by two separate guitars on the recording, but their call and response phraseology made an ideal combination part, especially if you happen to be the only guitar. In fact, when playing tunes that originally featured many guitars you'll often find it necessary to create "composite" parts that may even encompass keyboard or horn section parts.

Also of note here is the 16th-note shuffle rhythm, a double-timed version of the 8th note shuffle. Using alternate picking to lock into the 16th note shuffle groove, begin with both grace notes prepared (held without picking) with your 1st and 2nd fingers. As you pick, quickly hammer your 3rd finger on the G string, 10th fret. Next, slip down into the 6th position and nail the next double stop on the last 16th note of beat 1 (with an upstroke, natch!) and continue on for a repeat hit on the "and" of beat 2.

The notes on beat 4 imply B♭m and set you up for the rhythmic response in bar 10. The optional parenthesized "ghost notes" are barely played (sometimes only as a slight, muted "chick"). This 2-bar figure gets you through the majority of the tune.

The Bridge section uses a modulation (key change) to a single B^9 chord built to a crescendo over 4 bars of 16th notes (swing-16th's, remember!) before returning to B♭^{9} via a sharp accent on the last 16th note of beat 4. Since Stevie Ray Vaughan scat sings along with the bridge melody, try a little extra-curricular ear training and see if you can learn this part on your own.

The Cm^6 vamp during the Guitar Solo is another funky 16th note pattern and again the 1-bar rhythm motif repeats for the duration of this section.

Look for a few subtle additions during the repeated Outro section, but in general the parts remain the same.

Baboom/Mama Said

By Jimmie Vaughan, Stevie Ray Vaughan and Denny Freeman

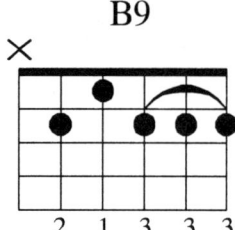

B9

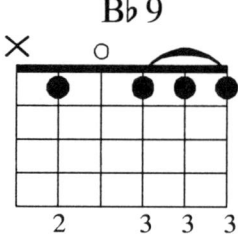

B♭9

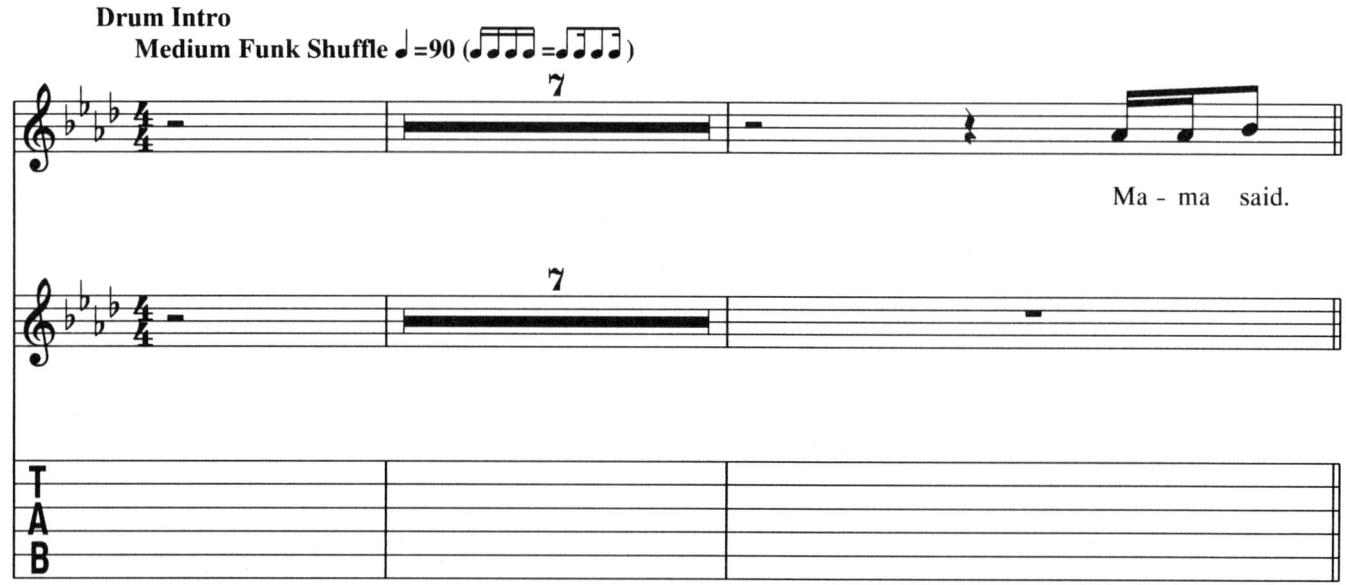

Drum Intro
Medium Funk Shuffle ♩=90

Ma - ma said.

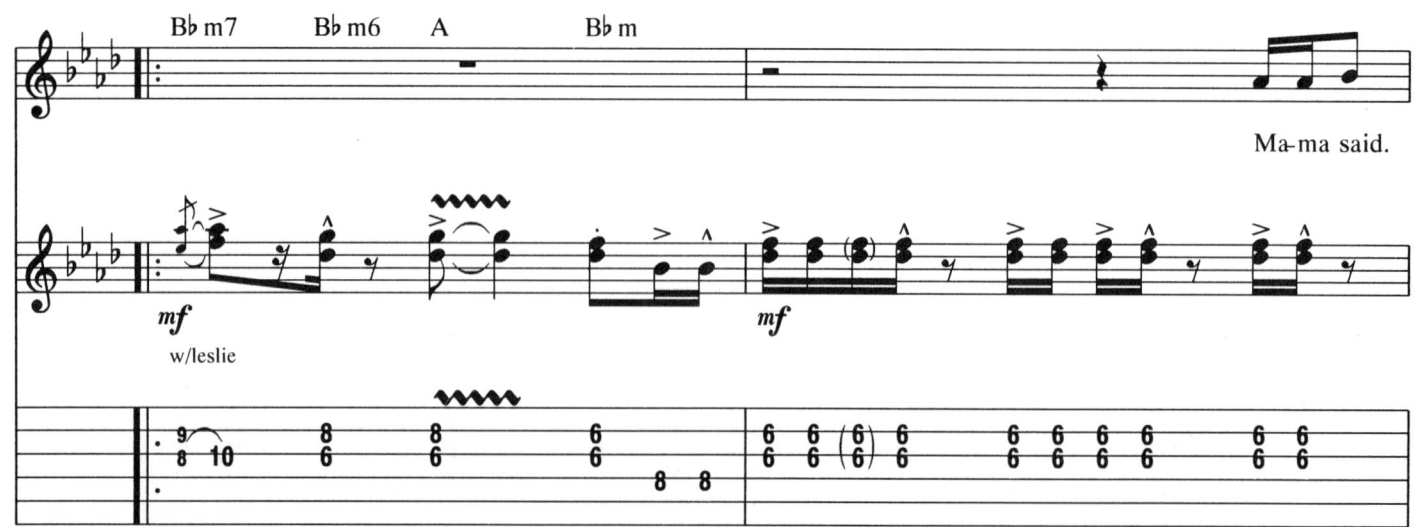

Ma-ma said.

w/leslie

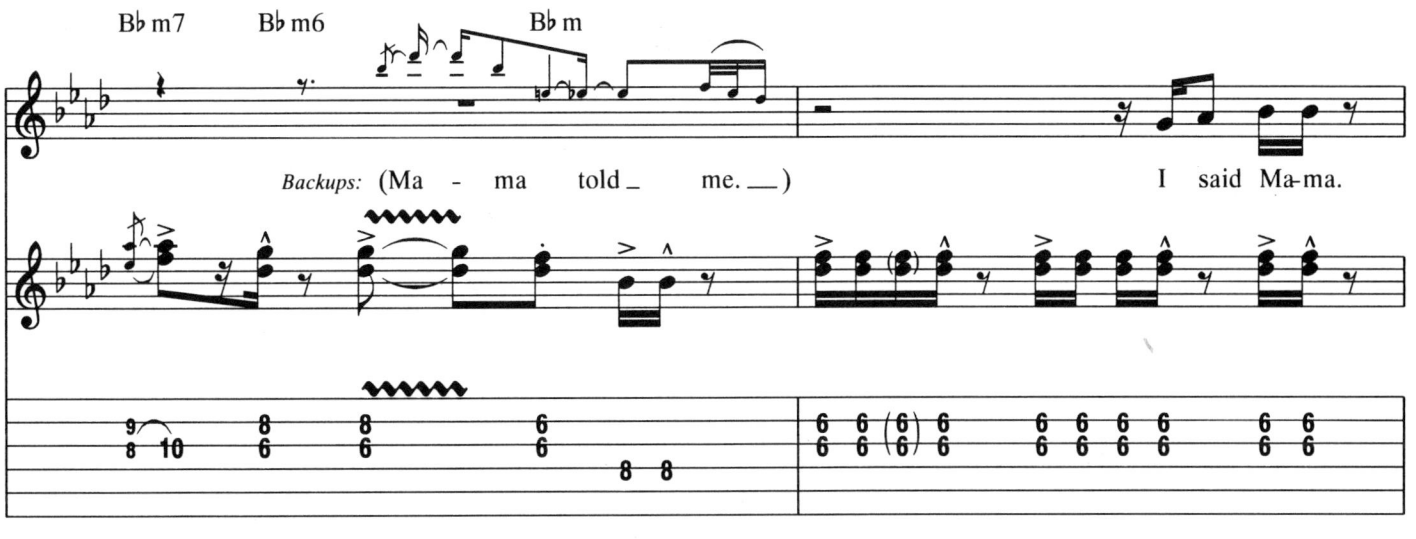

Bb m7   Bb m6   Bb m

Backups: (Ma - ma told _ me. _)   I said Ma-ma.

Ma-ma said.

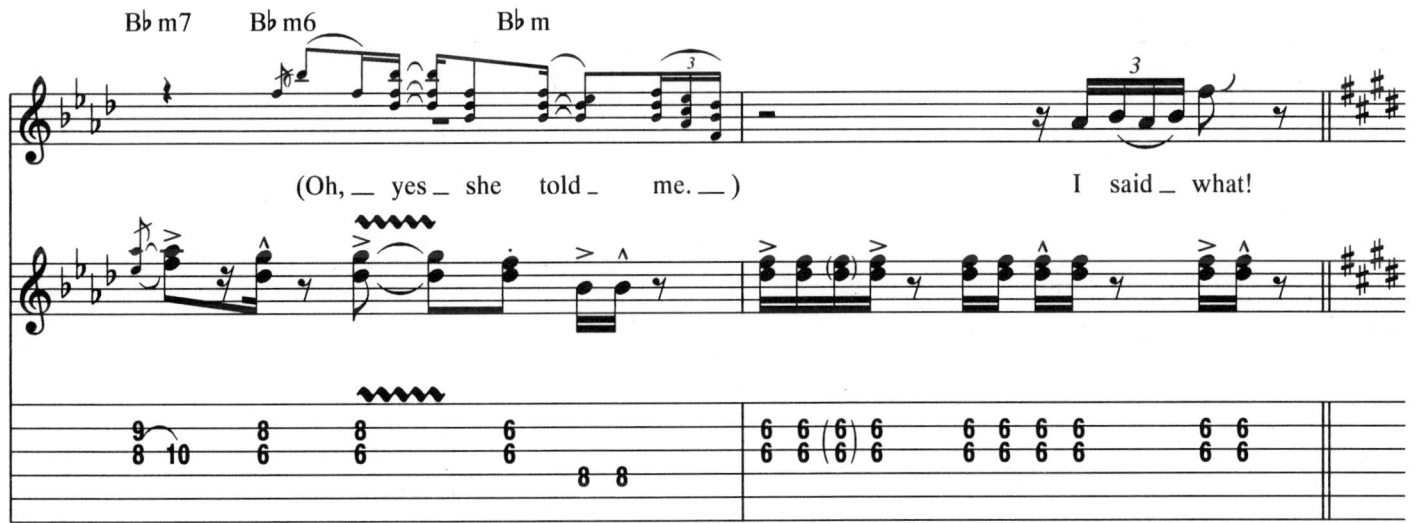

Bb m7   Bb m6   Bb m

(Oh, _ yes _ she told _ me. _)   I said _ what!

B mixolydian (B C# D# E F# G# A B)

B9

p   *grad. cresc.*

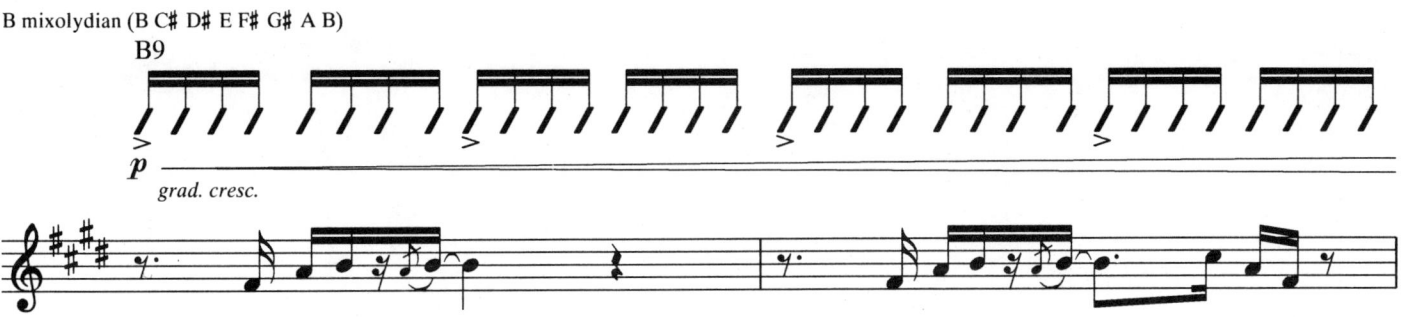

'N', da, da,   da, _   'n', da da,   da, _   da, da da.

'N', da, da, da, — 'n', da, da, da, — Ma-ma said.

Ma-ma said.

Ma - ma told — me. — I said Ma-ma.

Ma-ma said.

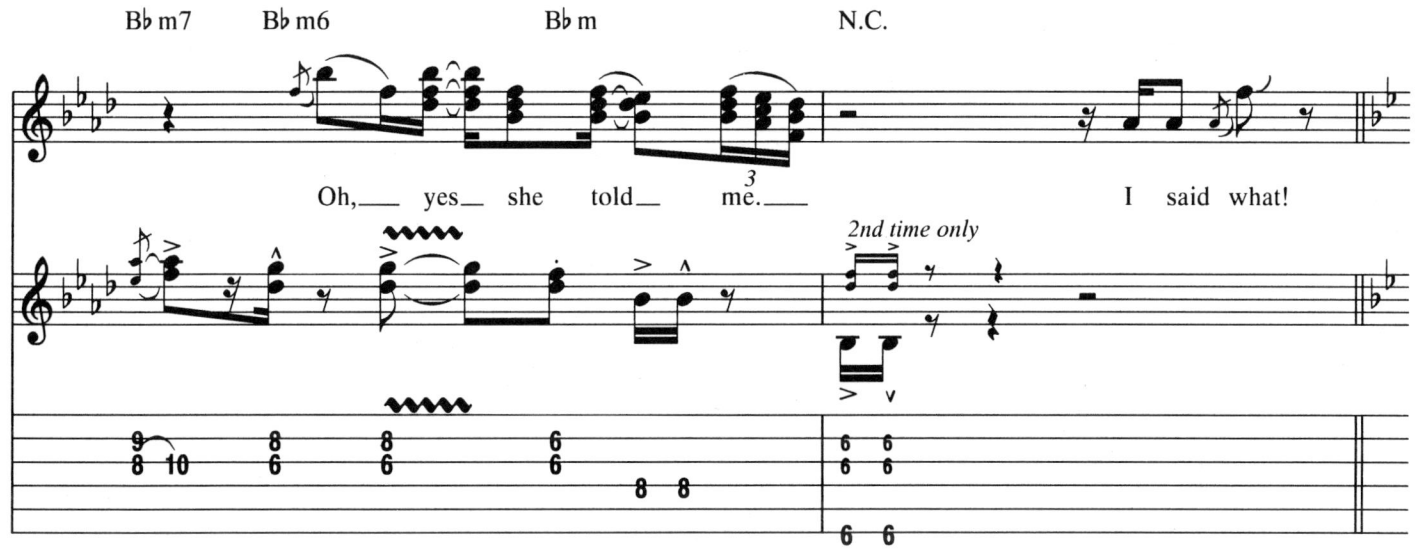

Oh,___ yes___ she told___ me.___   I said what!

Guitar Solo

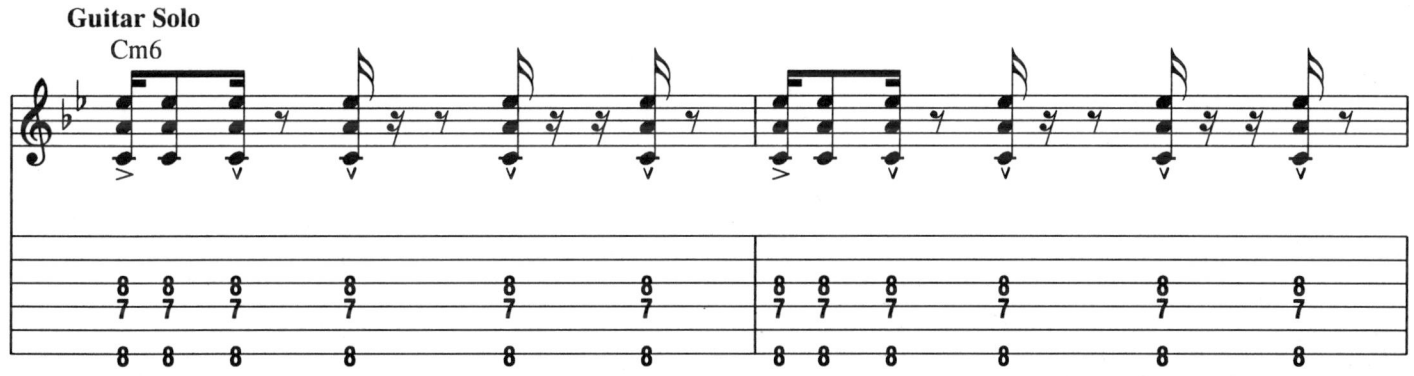

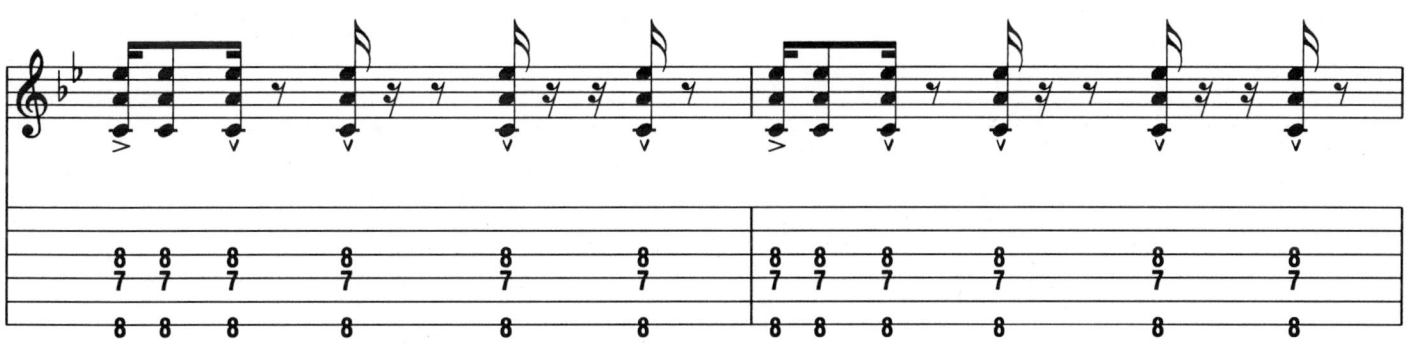

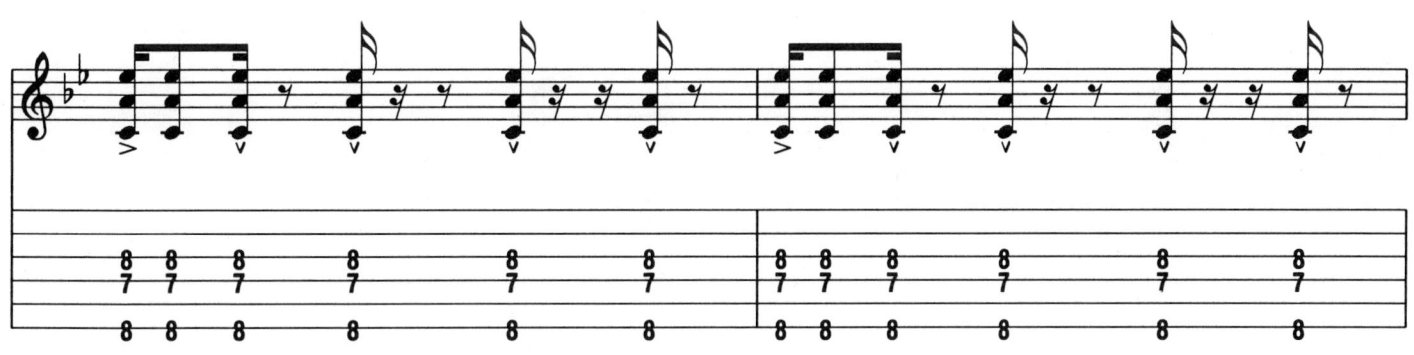

Verse

Ma-ma told_ me.___ I said Ma-ma.

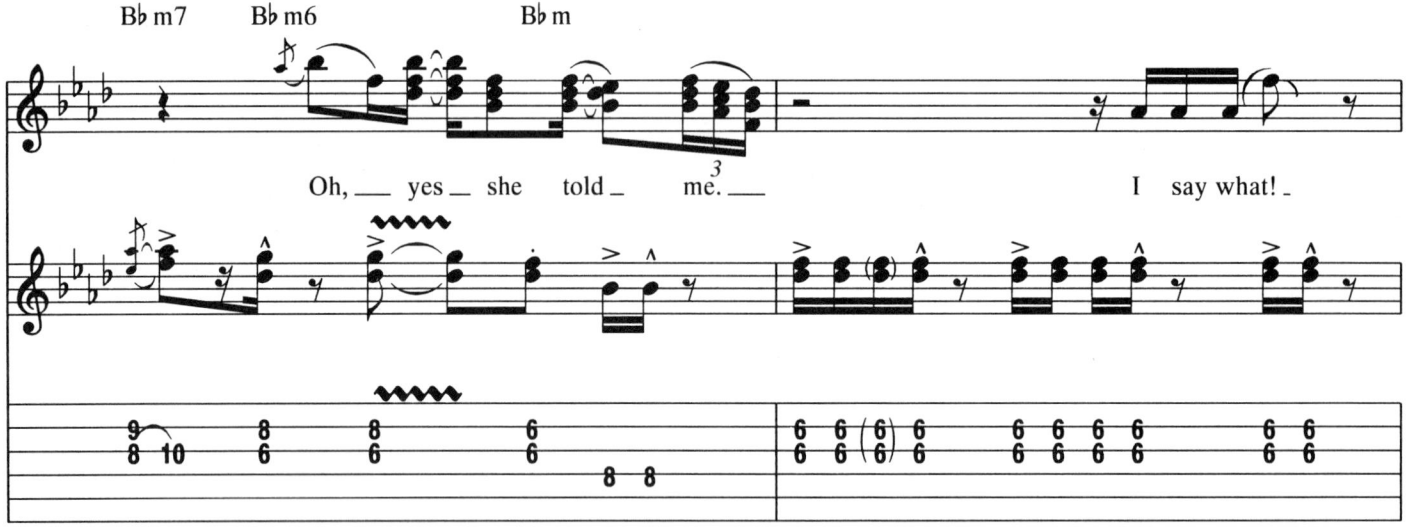

Oh,___ yes_ she told_ me.___ I say what!_

Gtr. tacet

Ma-ma. Ma-ma. Ma-ma. Ma-ma.

Ma-ma. Ma-ma. Ma-ma. Ma-ma said

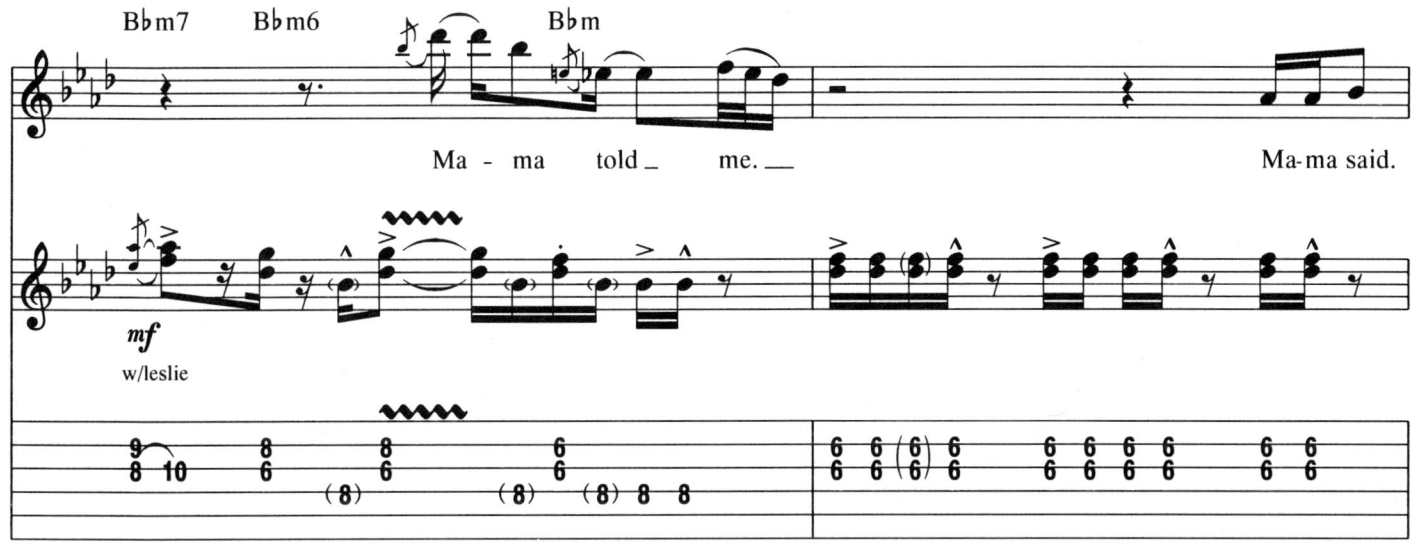

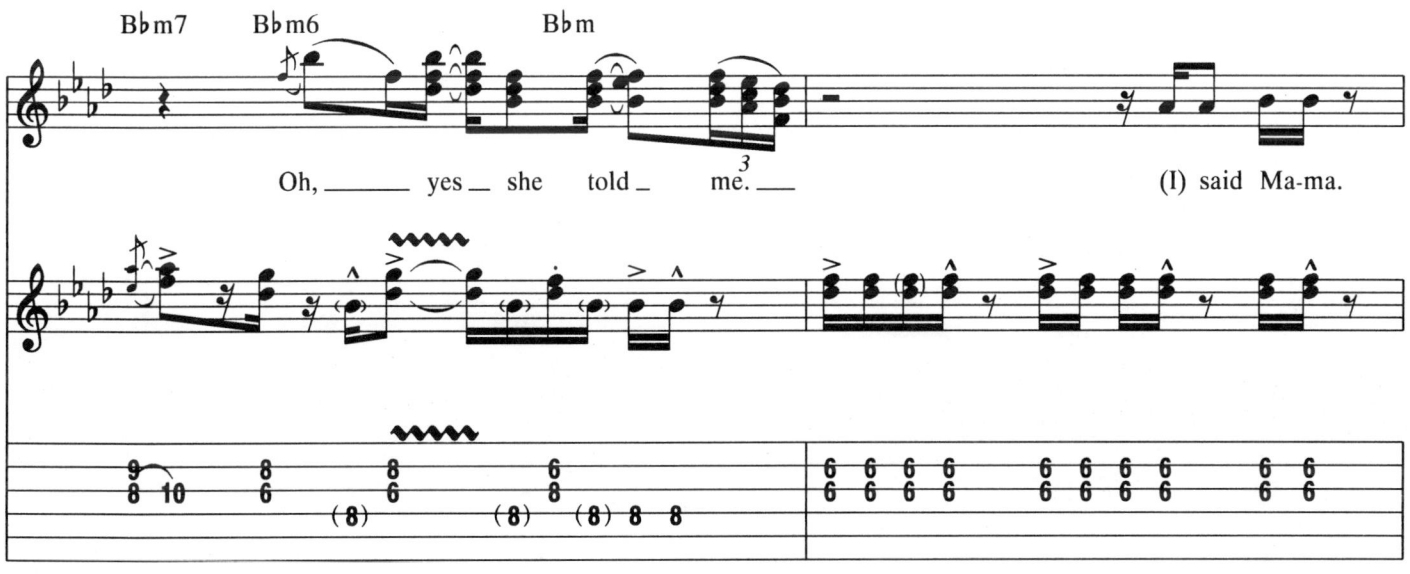

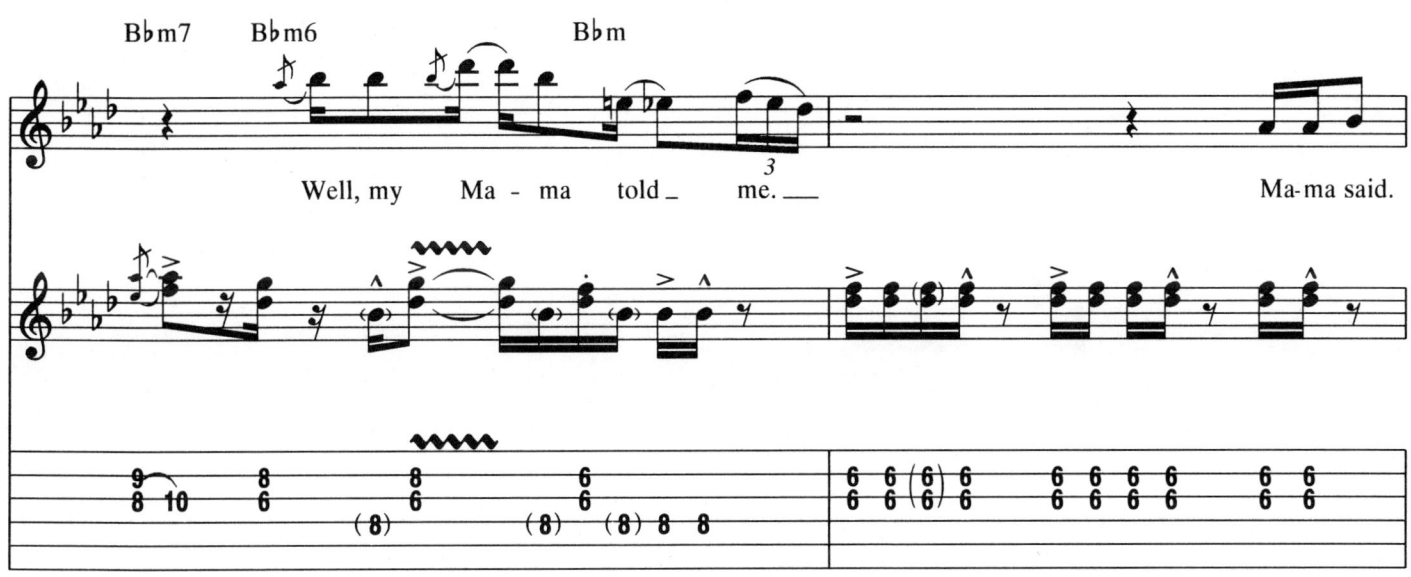

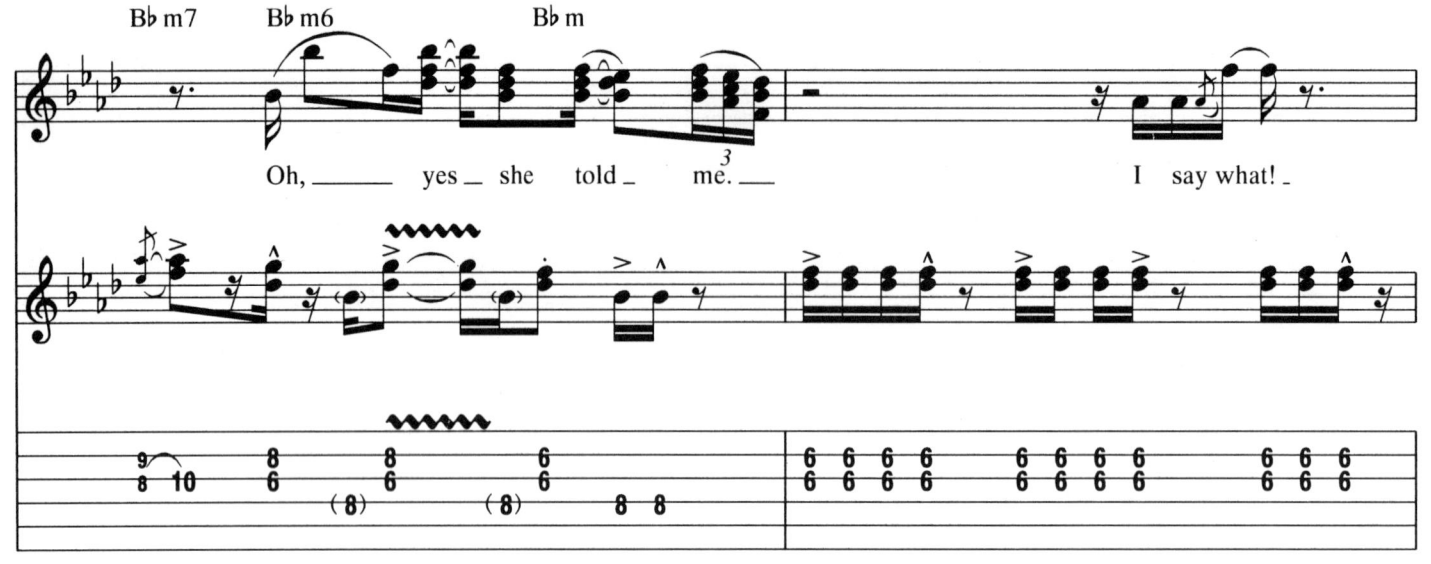

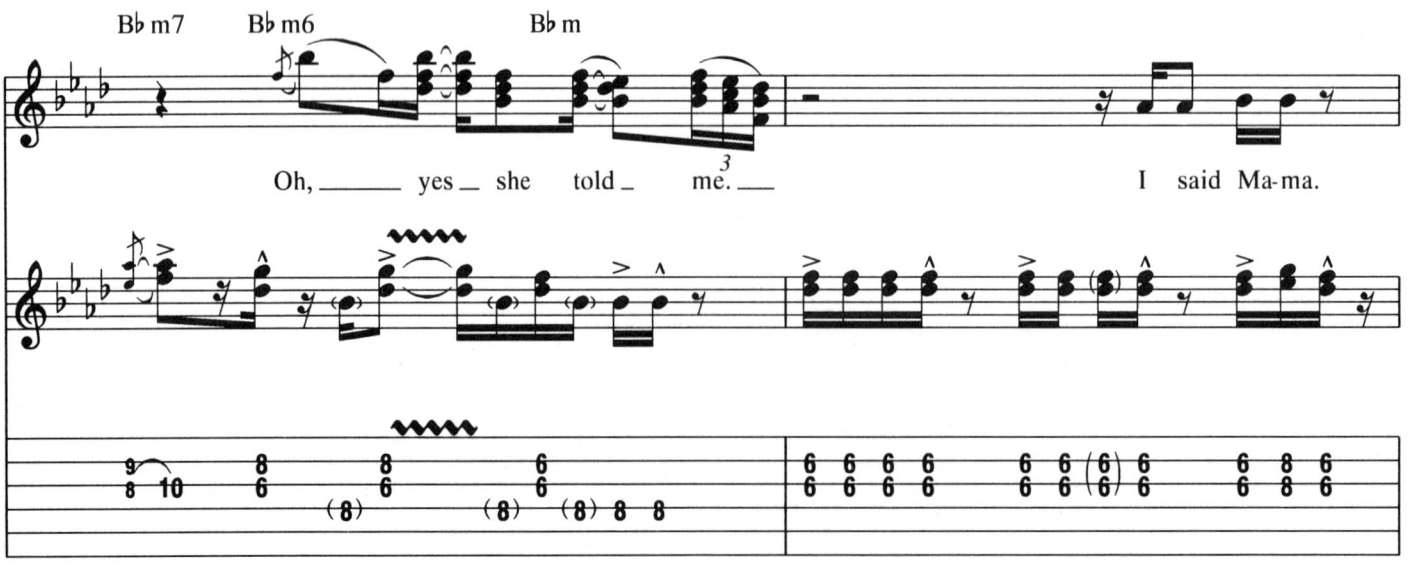

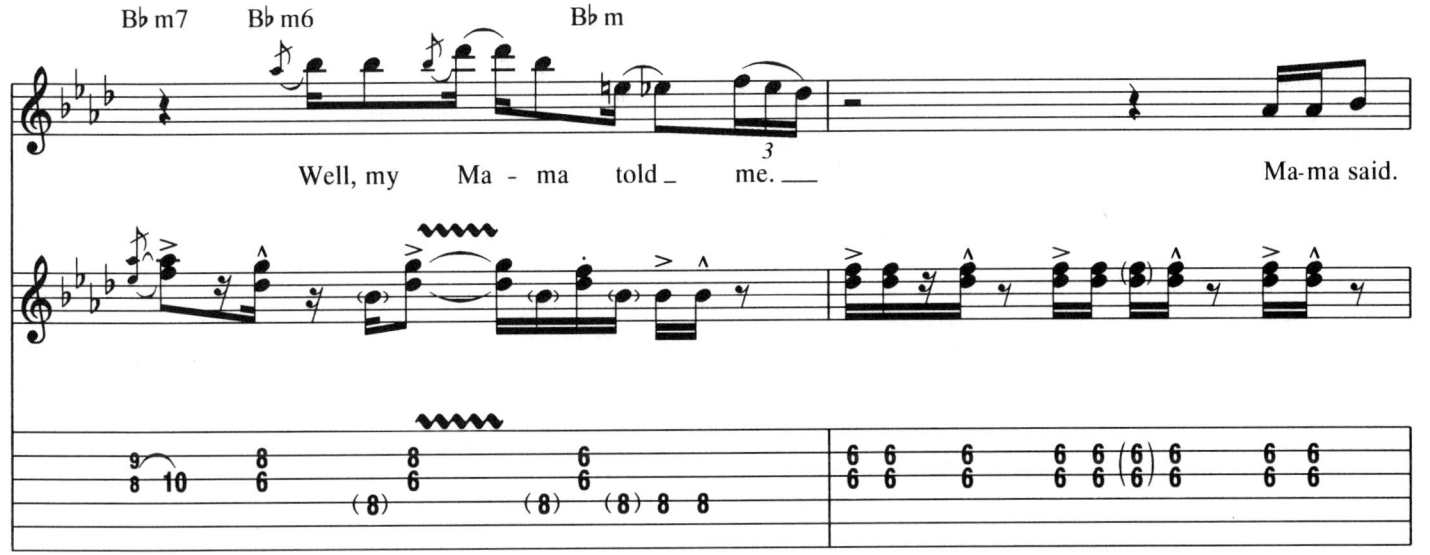

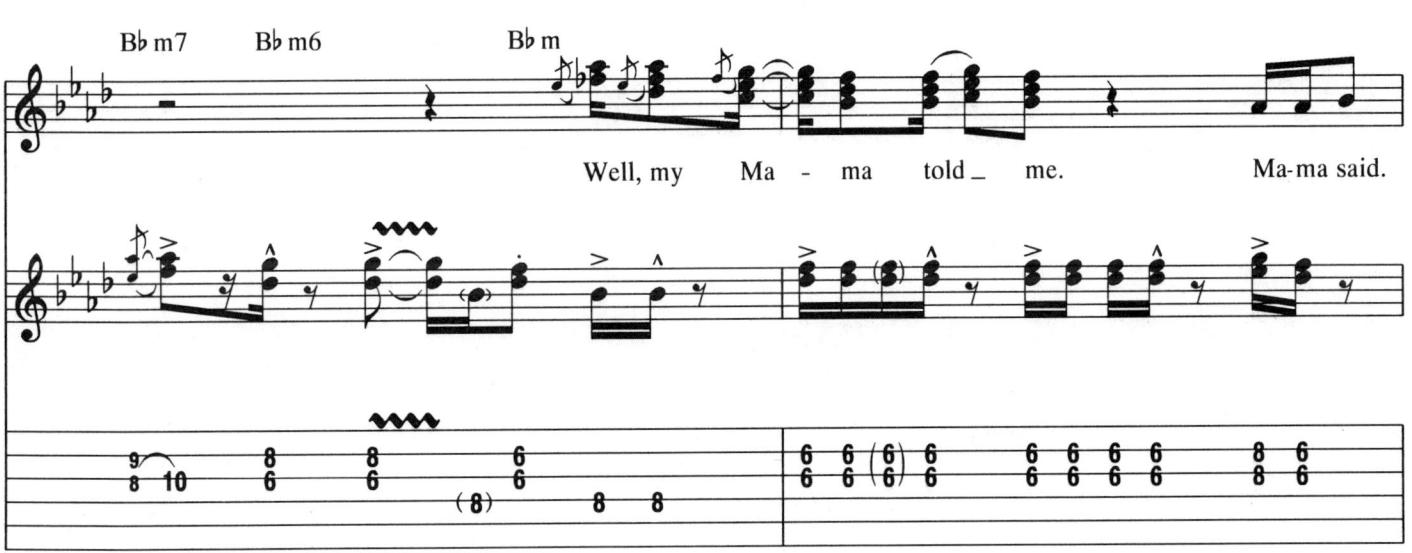

Well, my Ma - ma, Ma-ma said.

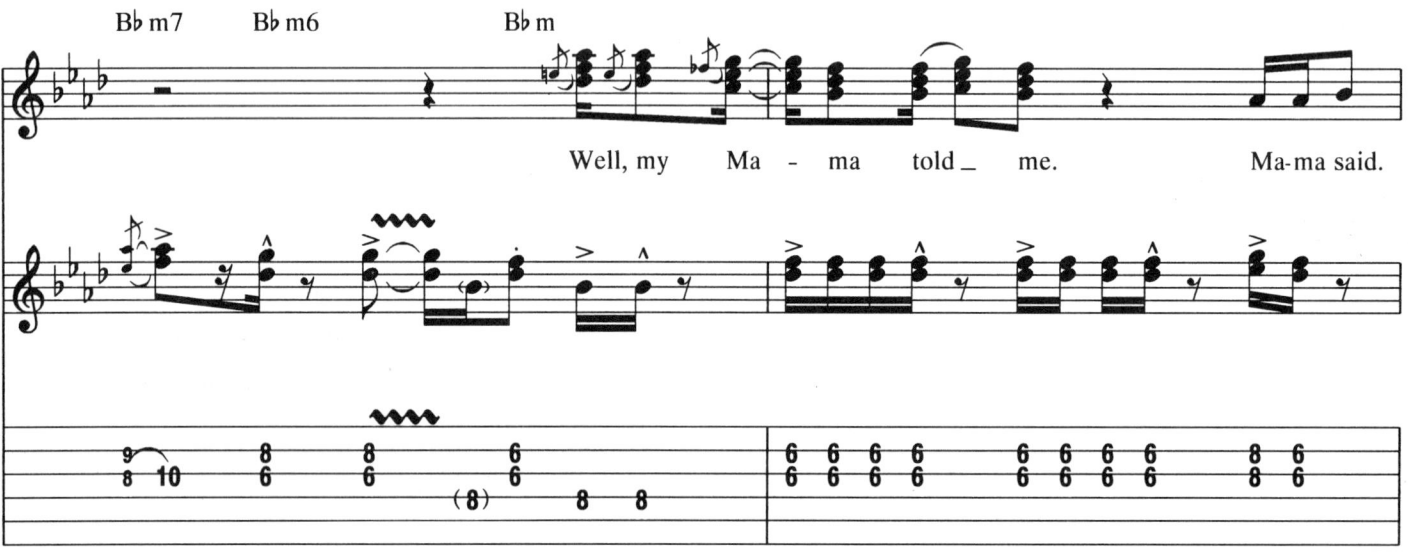

Well, my Ma - ma told _ me. Ma-ma said.

Fade

Well, my Ma - ma, Ma-ma said.

BROTHERS

LESSON

Since this tune is basically a long, slow instrumental blues jam, with only one guitar (being passed between Jimmie Vaughan and Stevie Ray Vaughan) throughout, we will take a rhythmic approach by arranging the accordian accompaniment through the 5th chorus for guitar. This 12-bar G blues uses a "quick change" to the IV chord in bar 2 of the progression:

$\frac{12}{8}$ I (G7)	IV (C7)	I (G7)	I (G7)
IV (C7)	IV (C7)	I (G7)	I (G7)
V (D7)	IV (C7)	I (G7) IV (C7)	I (G7) V (D7)

In 12/8 time, each beat is sub-divided into three 8th notes, making it, in effect, a very slow shuffle. Try creating your own rhythm figure variations using combinations of these rhythms with the written chord voicings.

The notes of the G pentatonic minor scale provide not only ample material for soloing, but can also be used to create bass register fills between chords. Here are two common G pentatonic minor patterns:

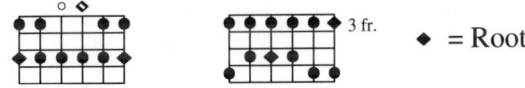

Study the single-note bass fills in the arrangement, then try adding your own variations.

Be sure to count through the chord breaks in the 3rd, 4th and 5th Choruses evenly, being especially careful not to rush. Don't hesitate to tap or pat the body of your guitar or the strings if it helps you to keep better time.

On the 6th Chorus, Jimmie Vaughan plays a repeated horn-section-like figure utilizing double stops, triple stops and single notes. Note throughout the progression that the I (G) chord figures include grace note hammers from the flat 3rd to the 3rd, while the IV (C) chord figures do not.

The tremolo-picking in bars 32 and 33 may be thought of as three 16th-note triplets per beat:

The ending lick is played almost exclusively using the G pentatonic minor scale. For the bends, remember to back up your 3rd finger and strive for accurate intonation (i.e., don't overbend or underbend!). Notice the B♯ (the only note not common to G pentatonic minor) at the very end. Once you get these ending licks down, you can try recycling some of them into your own solo choruses! the parts remain the same.

Brothers

By Jimmie Vaughan and Stevie Ray Vaughan

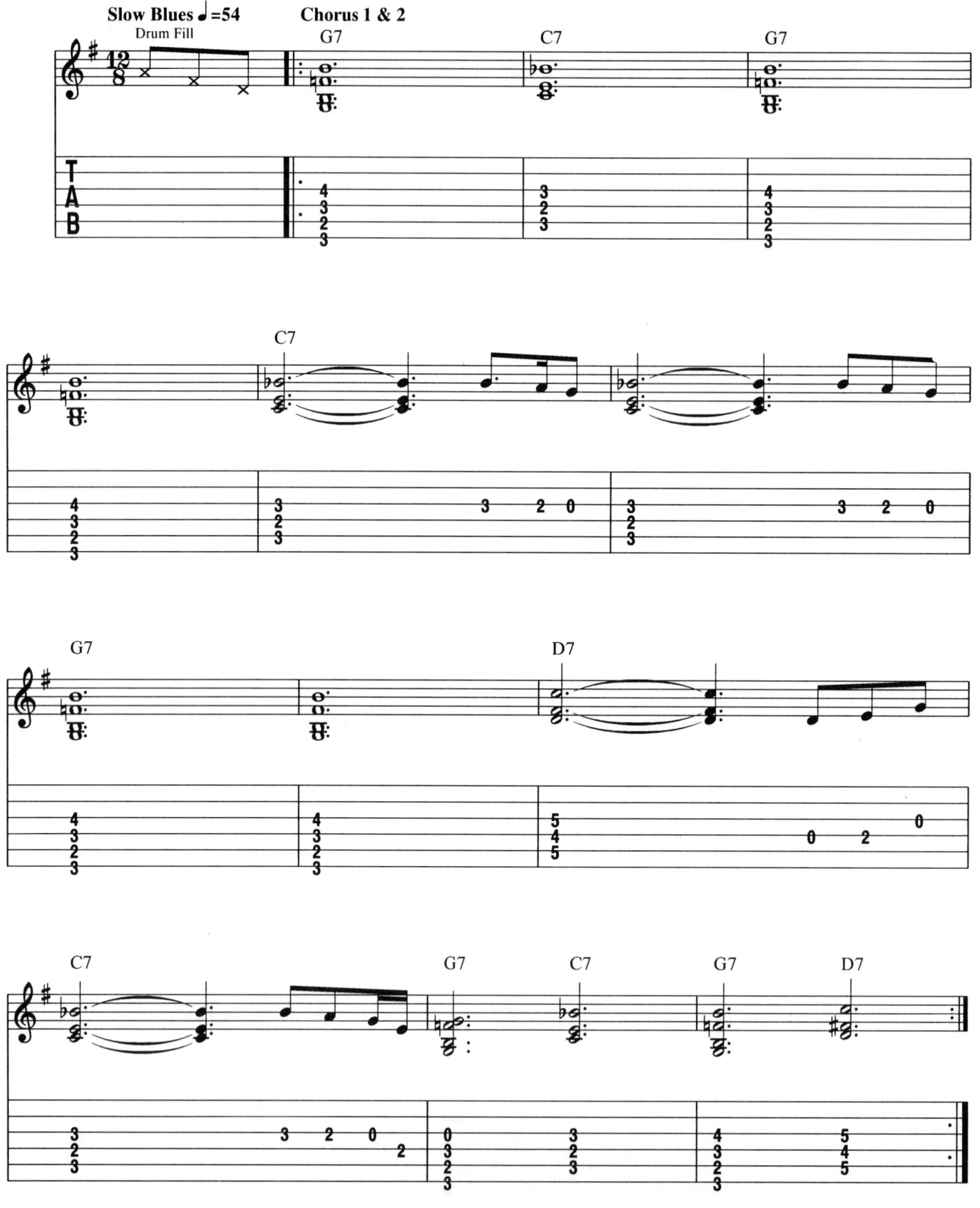

Chorus 3, 4 & 5

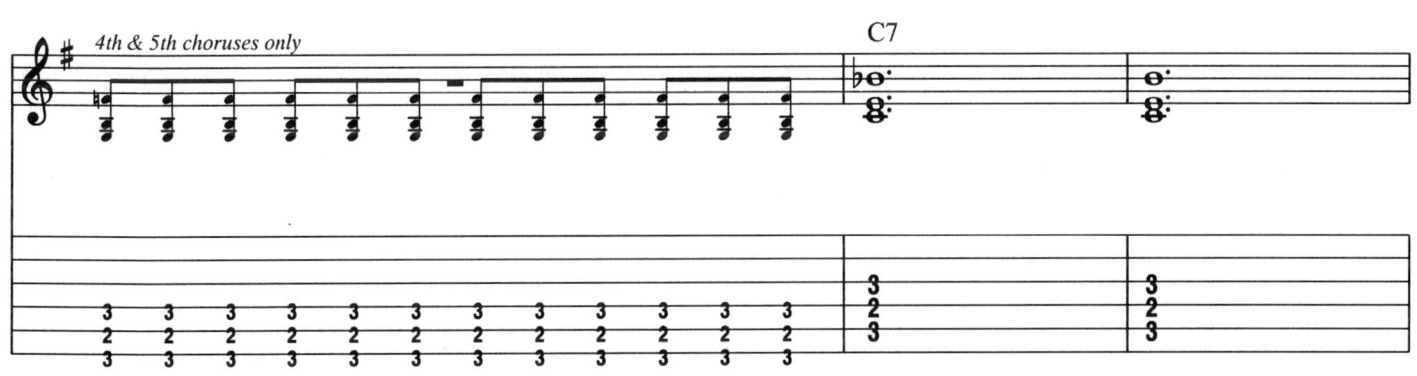

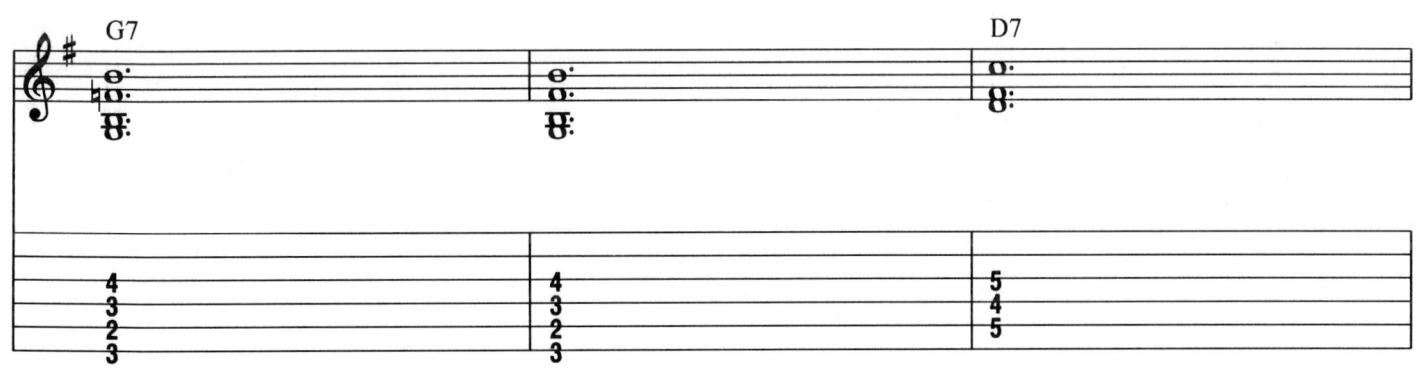

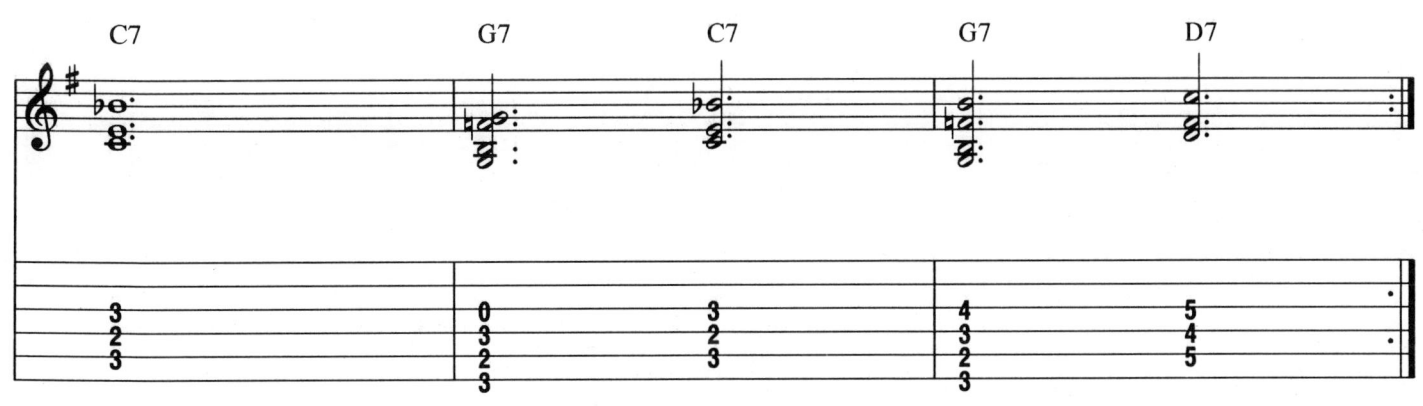

Chorus 6

Mm hmm, _ yeah! _

That sounds good! That's right!

Mm hmm. _ Boys, _

sounds good!

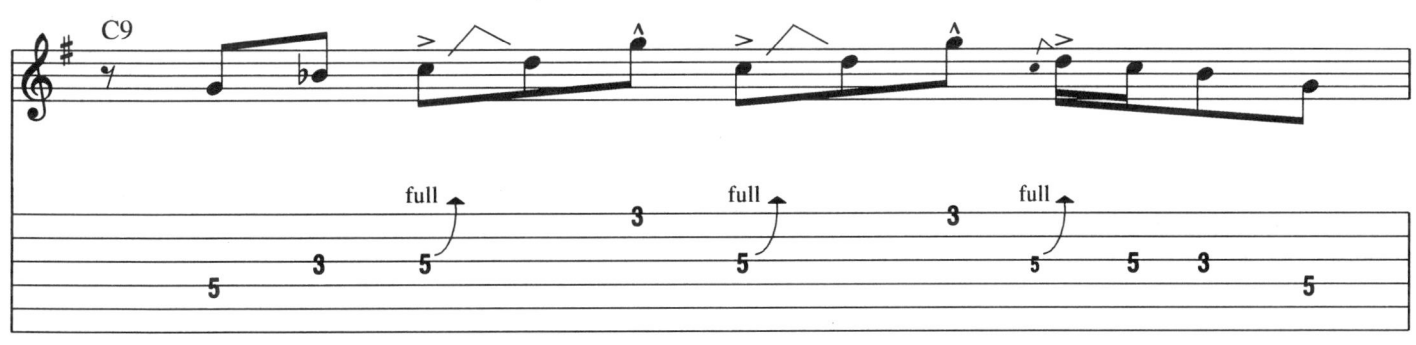

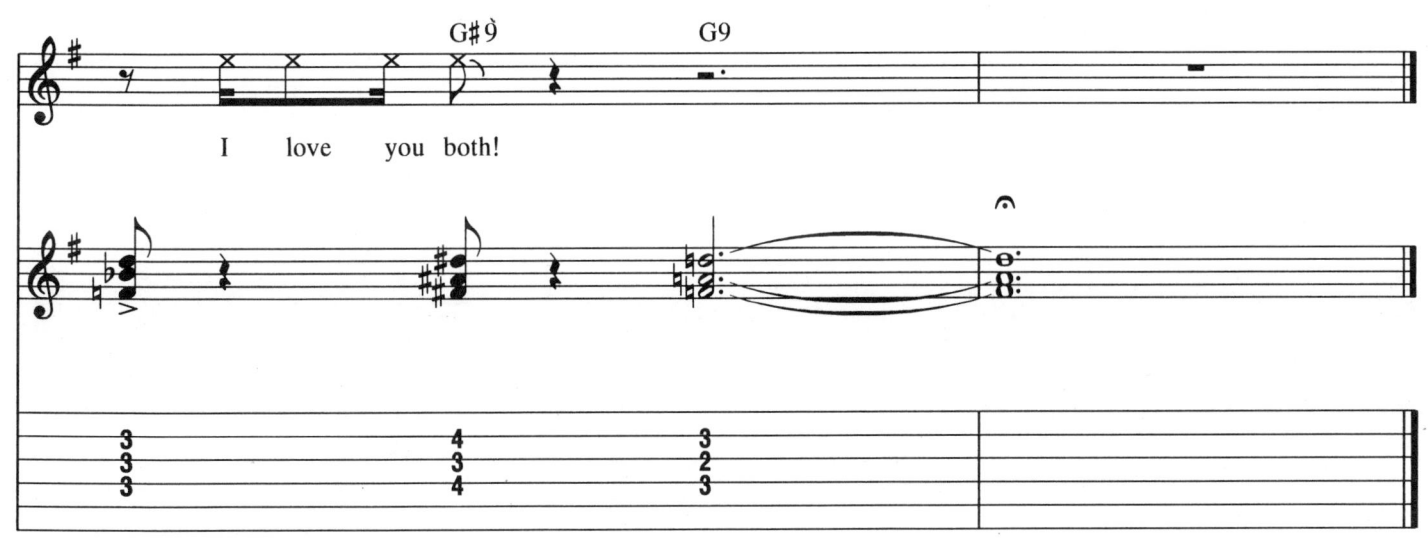

I love you both!

NOTATION LEGEND